Y0-CBC-100

THE WAR
IS BELIEF

THE WAR
IS BELIEF

Winning the
Most Important Conflict
in Success

By

JULIUS HENDERSON

Author of *The 7th Decision*

The War is Belief:
Winning the Most Important Conflict in Success
By Julius Henderson

Copyright©2008 by Julius Henderson
Published by You Publishing, El Dorado, California

You Consulting offer program and materials to help people improve their life and find their identity. For more information on our coaching programs, seminars, audio tapes, and books visit us online at www.iamyouinc.com or www.juliushenderson.com

All right reserved. No parts of this publication- text or pictures-maybe reproduced, stored in a retrieval system, or transmitted in any form or by any means-electronic, mechanical, photocopy, digital, broadcast, or any other-except for brief quotation in printed or broadcast reviews, without prior permission by the publisher.

ISBN 978-1-60530-539-4

FIRST EDITION / FIRST PRINTING
Printed in the United States of America

CONTENTS

9   **BONUS BATTLE** *Protecting Yourself from Belief Viruses   97*

To Precious...

I left my sister's house with the realization that the shell of my sister's body was all that was left. She fought a valiant battle to survive, to remain amongst the living. She was gone—her spirit, her support, her loyalty to me as a big sis, and her devotion to her family as a wife, daughter and mother. Despite my talents, I was confused at times in life, but she was always there, encouraging me, crying for me, and worrying about her little "Fudd," as she called me. I'm an introvert by nature. I think alone, cry alone, worry alone, but she had the key. She could walk through a door and demand attention. That was an earned characteristic of our relationship. I trusted her explicitly, not because she was always right, not because she was always reasonable, not because she was always on my side, but because she always believed.

She always believed in me. When I was on high, she believed in me; when I fell to the floor, she still believed; when I faced the repercussions of stupid decisions, she believed; and when I tried to balance out this adult thing, she kept believing. We would fight like a civil war and make up just by sliding back in each other's life, never mentioning the fight. When she became sick, she asked me to come help her navigate some decision-making. As it became evident she would lose this battle, I sank behind the lines of being seen, back to my corner, to being alone. We talked frequently during the weeks, but never talked about what would happen when she left this fragile existence.

When we came to the final days, the whole setting took on a life of its own. Many friends and family surrounded the house, and my strong mother looked powerless as she moved gently from my sister's room to holding her granddaughter. Seeing my mother facing that level of pain could move one to curse God for playing this practical joke called life on us. If it weren't for my strong biblical upbringing and my Southern mother's quick backhand, I might have voiced that.

On October 30, 2006, Precious slipped into death's sleep surrounded by those she loved and in her mother's comforting presence. The greatest pain is to feel nothing, and as her body was removed from the house, I felt absolutely numb. After the memorial, I returned home and stayed in my house for days, thinking about the coming days without my sister, missing her infectious laugh, her budging eyes when she's excited and our long phone conversations in which I update her about my progress and setbacks in life and business. As days passed, my tears dried up and the sun slowly came up, but the stars would never be the same because my greatest star was lost. I dedicate the words in this book to my greatest fan, my sister Yolanda "Precious" Putnam.

PREFACE

Las Vegas 2007

I facilitated a workshop with an all-female group of highly successful entrepreneurs, all from different walks of life, different generations, different religious beliefs, and of course different thought patterns. In the discussions, the women's separate backgrounds were evident from the way each digested and commented on different issues raised. As in any discussion where the participants are from disparate backgrounds, there were differences which on later reflection, turned out to have benefitted the discourse. As the diverse thoughts, which the group respected and digested, collided, the power of the subject matter broadened. The collisions also exposed blind spots in each individual's mentality and enhanced the participants' perception immensely.

As time passed, it became evident that these powerful women shared a unity, without which their varying perspectives would have led them into a valley of indecision. This unity hinged on one factor—*belief*. It also became evident that their shared concept of belief was the culture that held them tightly as one, and that this concept had helped them weather generations of tests, generations of competition, and generations of a changing landscape in business and humanity.

It was at that seminar that I fully appreciated the central concept the seed of success needs to grow and to continue growing. That concept hasn't changed since the inception of the human race. It is riddled in the foundations of our differing spiritual beliefs, our differing families telling differing stories to children. It is at the heart of the world's economy and its education. It is the thesis in every folktale, the blood rushing in every sports franchise and in every founder who has made his or her audacious dreams a reality. That concept is simply, yet profoundly *belief*. It is the war that spills over onto every level of success, every level of life. Although times will send different battles, one can never forget that the only war that matters is the war of belief.

SIMPLE IS STILL PROFOUND

"I just believe, you have to believe, and it takes belief." As I advance in my journey toward fulfilling my goals, I think about the many comments I have heard throughout the years. "Come on. It can't be that simple." I decided to sue a corporate behemoth when those around me ran, ducked, and dodged for cover. After the settlement, those that ran came back with the usual question, "How did you do that?" "I just believe, you have to believe, and it takes belief." That simple answer left those that ran perplexed. They wanted something more, something miraculous, an answer that sounded visibly tangible and profound.

When I decided to quit my job and pen my first book, some college buds said I didn't have anything to say, while others said I didn't know enough to say anything. After it was written and appeared in *First for Women* magazine and after I did some television interviews, both groups wanted to know how I did that. I gave them my usual reply, "I just believe, you have to believe, and it takes belief." That answer was too simple for both groups; they wanted something more miraculous, an answer that was more visibly tangible and profound.

In all of my challenges I believed, through all of my mistakes I believed, when setbacks surfaced, I may have been in tears, but I believed, when people deserted me, I may have been lonely, in despair, in pain, but I still believed. When folks in my circle gossiped behind my back, told me I was wasting my time, laughed at my dedication and were too embarrassed to stand when times were rough, I may have felt like I was nothing, I may have been embarrassed, I may have hidden from them, but I still believed.

That is why Las Vegas 2007 was so profound. It brought me back to the simple slogan that creates profound differences in each individual life. It was a shared realization, a confirmation in the highest sense that, yes, it does work, that belief is the thread that holds everything else together. But is it that simple? Was it simple belief that propelled Walt Disney to success although beginning with a mere $40 dollars in his pocket? Was it simple belief that propelled Mary Kay Ash's $5,000 life savings into a billion dollar Cosmetics Empire? Was it simple belief that made two young boys, William Harley and Arthur Davidson, who wanted to get to their favorite fishing spots faster, decide to create a motorized bicycle to do it? Was it simple belief that made Asa Candler, a partner in a successful small drug retail company, to the dismay of his friends, sell his entire stock of drugs, paints, oils, glass, and fancy clothes, all to invest in a strange formula made in someone's backyard by the weird name Coca-Cola?

Is belief that simple? And if it is, why does it have such a profound effect on those that manage to believe? Rosa Parks wasn't a strong person by stature; why did belief give her the power of Hercules as she took that seat on that bus defying the law of the land, not shivering at the eyes of those appalled and disgraced by her stance? And was it the same simple belief that gave Martin Luther King, Jr., then a skinny 26-year old kid, the standing of Gandhi as he emerged onto the national scene to come to her rescue? It couldn't be that simple, I thought to myself on my flight heading back home. Can simple be that profound?

YOUR LIFE WILL NEVER BE THE SAME

Prior to leaving Las Vegas, both individuals who organized the event, told me something that forced me, to think about belief.

On separate occasions, they relayed the same message, "Well Julius, your life will never be the same." Now these successful business women weren't referring to money. They have been successful for many years themselves. For five of those years, I've heard them train and talk about success and never have they highlighted money. They share Oprah Winfrey's belief, one of her ten personal commandments, that if money is your motivation, forget about it. So for them to tell me my life will never be the same entailed something far deeper, was more divining than the influence of money. What would change, I pondered, what door have I walked through that will alter all the others?

Settling back in my office, I found myself in a state of uncertainty, but this time there wasn't a crisis or set-back to pinpoint to explain this emotional low. What irony! Reality was saying, believe in yourself with unquestionable authority, while with the same force this voice of disbelief was ringing in my ear. I remember reading in Chris Gardner's autobiography, *The Pursuit of Happyness*, that after surpassing homelessness, and finally approaching an upswing in his life, Chris faced a second voice that suddenly entered the fray commanding unquestionable attention, a voice silencing his positive thoughts, speaking every negative and fowl word to his senses, a voice reminding him of why he wasn't deserving of the very success he was tangibly seeking by his own work.

I was perplexed when I read that experience in his memoirs, and more perplexed as my second voice entered the ring punching me senseless, ridiculing me with images of every mistake, regret, and setback I've ever encountered in life.

With pinpoint precision, it sought to excavate any remnants of positive imagery planted in my mind during my journey of success for the last ten years. My resume of change was rendered powerless by this loud threatening rendition of my darkest days. Like the villains in the comic books of my youth, it laughed slowly and arrogantly at my powers of positive attitude and affirmation. This went on for days as I walked around like Superman carrying a hand full of kryptonite, remembering the days of flight but stuck with this heavy weight of my past.

After a few nights with this irritating voice, I recalled the last episode of my Las Vegas trip. I was driven to the airport by the same two women who organized the event. I took mental notes of the pointers being given, consciously answering questions while subconsciously drifting into my own head wondering how a kid from Los Angeles, raised by a self-determined and no-excuses single mother, finds himself in a car with millionaires with families of different cultural backgrounds, women who have willingly and freely imparted their wisdom onto me and at the same time asked me to consult and train their successful colleagues.

As we pulled over at the terminal, and I grabbed my luggage, both women gave me huge hugs like proud parents, tenderly grabbed my face giving me a kiss of affection and each in their own words made a point. *Julius we believe in you, don't forget this moment, don't forget the responses of the people you trained, don't ever tire of your craft, of your dedication to what you do and above all **you believe in you.***

There is a way to overcome the struggle with my second voice, the kryptonite in my hands, which renders resumes and talents powerless and scoffs at positive thoughts and affirmations, the voice that has been lurking in me for a decade. That voice can only be silenced when I can affirmatively say in naked honesty that yes I believe in me.

My life would never be the same without the recognition that I truly believed in me. This is not a clichéd observation, but a surrendering to the me into whom I've worked diligently to evolve, the me I've always wanted, the me that justified Betty Henderson's sleepless nights, and battles with her children to want more and go after more, the me that required blood, sweat and tears to create.

This me upon acceptance would consciously allow me to walk through that final door, the door that muffles the sounds of the past. This me is what those successful women wanted me to grasp, the me they see, the me that is now truly me. After consciously surrendering to believing in me I, like Superman, sprung up and kicked that voice of disbelief out of the stratosphere. Oh, the villain will return, it knows me too well and loves sequels, but it has to return with a different plan and with mightier powers because Superman now has Superfriends.

CHAPTER 1

The War Is Belief

I am absolutely nothing. I cannot point you to anything fascinating about me, no formal education, no great financially backed upbringing with audacious goals of being placed front and center from infancy. In my youth, I made every mistake a young man can make. I've been as low as a person can go in his life and can comfortably relate to all people regardless of their view of life. I know rejection, embarrassment, shame, ridicule, failure, and personal confusion. Everything I have become and am in the process becoming is due only to one vicious conflict in which I've been engaged in for years, the war of belief.

Nothing is more potent in the realm of success than belief, nothing that can more effectively change the complexion of a life, the direction of a personal journey or the goals one sets. Confidence, self-esteem, finances, education, support, and opportunity come a distant second to the effects belief has on a person's life.

Belief in its truest form will alter how you see everything, it will sharpen your senses to excavate the deepest part of your very soul, it will force a grueling reshaping and remodeling process that is unlike anything else you will ever experience. It will illuminate your life and force you, everyone and everything out the shadows. If you didn't know, soon you will know; if you don't understand, soon you will understand. Belief will be your brightest personal flashlight, and it will shine on whatever is being internally concealed that is blocking you from your decided destination.

THE CONFLICTING POWER OF BELIEF

It is what belief does that causes the conflict. The belief that feminists had in the 60's caused the conflict with the male dominated power structure. Belief of those nine young African American youth in Little Rock, Arkansas caused its Governor to call out the National Guard to try to prevent them from entering an integrated school. Belief unified the heart of three priests, Edward Müller, Hermann Lange and Johannes Prassek, and an Evangelical pastor, Karl Friedrich Stellbrink. Arrested in 1942, for a common conflict against Hitler, the four men became good friends in prison and died together at Hamburg in November 1943. Their belief diminished their old denominational hostilities as they embraced their common cause, which lead them to their common fate.

"We are like brothers," Lange said of their relationship as Stellbrink stepped up to the guillotine.

Belief is so much more than passing affirmations and clichéd nuisances. Belief is everything if there is going to be anything in your desired future. Belief is the inescapable path that the legends of success in business, social crusades, and humanitarian efforts have walked, the ones whose beliefs in the face of opposing opinion bravely and courageously withstood ridicule, danger, embarrassment, critics, abandonment, and hostility. Belief ignited their bones and guided them home to their desired place.

By its very nature, belief creates conflict because each opposing sides truly believes. Hitler believed just as mightily as his oppositional critics, a racist believes just as mightily as a minority, and a male chauvinist believes just as mightily as his opposing female resisters. War is a conflict of two beliefs; only in comic books and 60-second attention spans are its complexities reduced to simplistic themes. Always remember that belief is not simple, and if you bring in a simple mindset to fight against change, you will lose.

INCOMPLETE BELIEF DOES NOT IGNITE THE WAR

The basic concept of belief is simple. In Webster it is just: "*A state or habit of mind in which trust and confidence is placed in something or a person.*" Everyone can believe, and everyone does believe in something. When I have sat in trainings on the subject of success and heard the facilitator tell me repeatedly to believe, I would subconsciously reassert to myself that I must be on pace because I am truly believing. With that confident focus, I thought I entered the war leading to change because the trainer highlighted that I was full of belief. Yet nothing changed.

Being in belief mode cannot be the "be all, end all" of success. I thought I was in belief mode but was, in fact, stagnant. There are other factors that you must consider.

In that incomplete belief mode, I tried to pursue my change, sharing my ideas with others in my immediate circle. I received nothing but supportive feedback, unaware at the time that all of my ideas had been formed with boundaries that prevented me from straying from the thoughts of the pack. So naturally my change was limited from inception.

I set powerful goals for myself, yet my agenda in carrying out those goals came with a commanding caveat, having to please people and avoid making waves. Naturally, I was in a tug-of-war with two conflicting yet very powerful ideas, which had me sweating as I pulled both ends but heading in no dominant direction. The tugs were real, as was my work; but the boundaries were real as well, as were the rules. So either I was crazy or there was another component to belief that I was overlooking.

BELIEF JUSTIFICATION SPARKS THE WAR

I entered the process of change armed with this basic concept of belief, the concept that only means to trust what I was thinking, trust the habits of my mentality, and trust the patterns of how I digested information and assembled my conclusion. This concept, although definitely a part of belief, was not what created the conflict, what sparked the war in which I am currently engaged, which has changed the surface of my life and altered the destination of my future. This was *justification of my belief.*

When I had this simple and noble idea that I wanted to become a better person, upgrade how I saw life, and aspire for freedom mentally, spiritually, emotionally, and financially, at first blush I thought the request would ignite an external venture, in which my only concerns would be which class to attend, which show to watch, and which book to read in order to come to—presto, a new life.

But as time went on and this external pursuit was not producing results, I asked myself a few very simple questions: Why do I believe what I believe about those very things I want to change? What went into shaping the very boundaries of the current beliefs with which I had lived my life? Why as an adult had I come to my conclusions? Why do I believe in my current concept of the most important things in my life, spiritually, financially, and mentally?

What I was asking was still within the context of belief, which again means simply, *"a state or habit of mind in which trust and confidence is placed in something or a person."* But what I was now addressing was a much heavier issue than the habit of my mind, more importantly why did I trust the sources that were instrumental in creating my habits of belief, habits of how I looked at things spiritually, financially, mentally? For the first time in my adult life, I was embarking on a complete understanding of belief, the meat of the matter— my justifications for the habits to which I have grown accustomed.

Justification (or justify) based on Webster means simply: *"to prove or show to be just, right, or reasonable."* Ask people what they believe or trust, and the masses can roll it off their tongues. Ask them how they justify their belief, and you'll hear the stutters. For the first time in my life, why I believed was more important to me than what I believed, but, unbeknownst to me, what I believed, my habit of mind, had created reasons to avoid discovering the justification for the belief.

JUSTIFICATION BUILDS A FORTRESS AROUND YOUR BELIEFS

Dorothy Thompson, called the first American woman of journalism, once quoted, *"There's nothing to fear but the persistent refusal to find truth, the persistent refusal to analyze the causes of happenings."* Reading this quote is powerful enough; living this quote is mind blowing. When I asked myself this question about justifying my beliefs, it was astonishing to face the fact that my life had been largely based on opinions. While some of those opinions turned out to be quite factual, I personally didn't know which of them were based on fiction and which on nonfiction. From this unclear data, my justifications were formed.

Now some of you may ask how can that be, how can you not know if something is factual if it has been a habit of mind for so long? The answer is that I was not engaged in my life; I was only engaged in the life already traced by the influence of those opinions. When I say traced, it reminds me of the times when coloring as a kid, I would start with a black crayon and darken the line of an image, creating a very dominant border-line. The rest of the bright colored crayons would be used to carefully finish the inside of the image, but I was well aware that I should skillfully and cautiously stay within the bound-aries of the black trace. That is what we called coloring when I was a kid. Fast-forward, and as an adult I was still coloring.

Others opinions created the trace, so regardless of my per-sonal ambitions, which were very colorful, I have lived most of my adult life well aware that I shouldn't stray beyond the mental borders. Now, my goals were pushing me beyond the borders, saying you must go beyond the justification of the trace. Yet the trace itself has justifying reasons not to cross; it has been there for years and has built a fortress around itself.

Fear stood alone as the most influential soldier protecting my belief that I should stay put. In itself, fear is a formidable justification for people to keep their mental habits. A clichéd form of belief is not going to break the powerful influence of this soldier. Remember, it is the trace that fear protects, not the embodiment of the picture. This soldier is not protecting the conversation that individuals may be having about some-one else. It's only interested in blocking them from seeing the irony of their own justification.

It is not concerned with the idiosyncrasies of others that an individual can pinpoint with skilled accuracy; it ensures the habit of mind that allows the same person to justify sitting in the same idiosyncrasies. It is not concerned with a person's discussion of his or her boss, it blocks that person from taking the initial step to free him or herself from that which the person hates. It allows us to be objective and tell others precisely what they need to do and then blocks us from exerting ourselves to do those very same things. Fear was not protecting me from seeing where others would end up if they didn't change their habits of mind; it blocked me from seeing where I was heading with my current mental habits.

Other things also protected the justification that kept me within the trace, including memories of mistakes, failure, shame, embarrassment and financial concerns. These all very real things ensured that staying within the walls of the trace was not only doable, but sensible as well. No one could have convinced me that my reason for staying put wasn't sound. No one could have helped me break through that wall. I needed something to absorb the mental and emotional blows of deviating from the trace. I needed a need.

NEW DESTINATION MAKES WAY
FOR NEW JUSTIFICATIONS

If given a chance to take a trip into your past for a 15-minute conversation with yourself at the ripe age of twenty-one, getting set to embark on life's choices, just you sitting down with you with the knowledge you have of life today, and knowing that conversation would alter the life you live now, what would you talk about? What would you tell yourself? How would you respond to the twenty-something you that is hearing what you're saying yet keeps interrupting wanting to focus on concerns about low self-esteem and friends' opinions?

How will you respond when you tell you that what you're talking about is nonsense, that your twenty-something friends and close family understand where you're coming from, and that they will never support you? Can you imagine your conversation? I can surely imagine my conversation.

NowJulius: Hey, I only have a couple of minutes I need to talk with you . . .

ThenJulius: Come on, man, my friends are waiting. We're going out.

NowJulius: Listen kid, forget them. Start right now focusing on upgrading with some new friends.

ThenJulius: New friends? You must be out of your mind.

NowJulius: Where are they going? What are they reading? Who are their friends? This is serious. Your choices right now will alter everything for us, right now.

ThenJulius: Oh, come on old man, with that ancient speech.

NowJulius: Did you start working on that business you were talking about?

THEN JULIUS: No, cancel that. I told some folks I know, and they didn't think that was cool.

NOW JULIUS: See, right there. That's what I'm talking about. Do not allow others to deter you that quickly. This is why I'm telling you to upgrade with new friends. Besides, what are they doing? What goals do they have? Huh, did you think about that?

THEN JULIUS: No, I didn't think about that.

NOW JULIUS: They're all following the leader, and the leader hasn't a clue. Hey, people have called you many things, stubborn, crazy, confused, but one thing about you, kid, you're no coward, you can take a stand alone, and that's what needed if you're going to have any life. Now, about those goals . . .

THEN JULIUS: But I don't have any money; people are going to be laughing at me if I fail.

This is when I reach out and grab my face to look myself straight in the eye.

NOW JULIUS: Listen, it's all an illusion, what you're saying right now about what you don't have is all an illusion. What's real is making that decision to go for it. I'm telling you, people who laugh and criticize are usually in a group and they are the gutless ones. I know you don't know that now, but life will unfold that reality out to you in due time.

THEN JULIUS: But I don't have anything, man. I have nothing to start with.

NowJulius: Start with tweaking that conversation. You
need to dig in those books, find people who have
done it, get to the source of all information, listen
with eagerness and believe only after verification.
Don't expect group participation, success in anything
is usually obtained in single digits. And lastly, quit
wearing those shoes, they're made for $5.00 and are
marked up 1000%.

Fifteen minutes is a lifetime when it is a conversation that
can alter your life. That exercise is a demonstration of how
talking points with ourselves change when we truly believe in
the outcome, the destination we seek. Conversations tend to
focus on need rather than want, substance rather then mental
sweeteners. "If I had a chance to do it over again," we say to
ourselves with hindsight being 20-20, no doubt we would zero
in on moving ourselves to another destination, and that would
become the most essential issue in the discussion, our destination. With that comes a reexamination of our justifications.

Remember, the basic incomplete version of belief is to
trust your habits of mind. When I look back at those around
me at the time of my metamorphosis, we had similar habits of
mind and similar beliefs, trusting in our habits of mind without asking why we trust them. We never asked that question,
we just gave each other reasons to keep current mental habits.
No one dared to question why we are on this mental merry-
go-around, spinning, trusting, and turning over life, time, and
energy? But we could not justify all in which we believed, and

worse yet, the fortress that had been built around our psyches prevented us from even wanting to dig to find out.

When I began to change, I went back and forth trying to convince people to look, investigate, question, which left me stagnant and exhausted. But things became clear to me when I read a piecing quote saying, "*Give a person who wants to be free one tool and they will use it to excavate themselves, give a person who wants to be a slave 14,000 tools they will keeping asking you for more.*" Bingo! I asked myself, what has carried me through the ups and downs? What has caused me to stand when others walked away? It was that I wanted freedom, my destination.

All conversation in convincing others is meaningless when destinations differ because in reality we are all justifying our destination. The people closest to me couldn't see what I was telling them due to the simple fact that they were destined to be where they were and I was destined not to be.

But were they given a chance to return to have a conversation with themselves at an early stage in their lives, their conversation would be different. I know they would tell their young selves not to focus on fear, to question everything, to go after that dream, not to listen to friends and family. I know they would look themselves straight in the face and say, forget about the past, forget about what didn't happen, forget about those who don't believe. I know they would because they would have physical, provable, and tangible evidence that had already lived and a new destination would make a difference in their lives now. A new destination is worth questioning, altering and reexamining justifications for their beliefs.

Destination is the battlefield of the war. It is why the war of belief even exists. Destination induces people to go against the grain of their comfort and do things others would think impossible. Destination is self-respect; Rosa Parks proudly sat where she wanted on that segregated bus, damn the consequences. Destination is a greater cause; Edith Stein stood up to the dictatorship of Hitler, damn the consequences, and she was executed for her stance. Destination is no one's statistic.

It took Chris Gardner from homelessness, to Dean Witter, from Dean Witter to Gardner International Holdings, damn the consequences. Destination is self-right. Mary Kay Ash created a company for women about women from scratch in a male dominated system, damn the consequences. A new destination that is vivid, bright and real that burns in the soul of an individual will open that person up to the possibility of exchanging justifications.

THE JUSTIFICATION EXCHANGE

Just as a matter of review, an incomplete belief is just a surface habit of mind. In real time it may sound like this. You are asking a colleague with a specific talent in a certain aspect of his life to pursue his dream, and he replies, "I can't make it." Yet when asked why, (the justification), he says, "I just know I can't make it." The habit of mind has been repeated so much it has basically justified itself.

A person is telling you something he has rendered to be truth, you then asked why that is truth, justify it, and the person says just because. The habit of mind has been repeated so much it has basically justified itself. You have been telling yourself something for years, yet you have no way of justifying it; it just feels correct. It is the habit of mind that has been repeated so much it has basically justified itself.

When you have a habit of mind without justification, your first impulse may be to set yourself straight with "the right and wrong remedy," but is that the most effective remedy? Is telling someone he or she is wrong about a habit of mind going to change the habit? Do you know how many people know it is wrong for their bodies to consume a diet of fast food, to persist in repeating their past mistakes, and to continue their negative self-talk, yet regularly engage in those very things?

I think the most powerful lesson within the walls of the scriptures is that the very people who waited for the Messiah, had the scrolls to direct them to his coming, and prayed fervently for his return, refused to believe when he did appear, as the scrolls prophesied, with miracles in hand. The habit of mind of worthlessness, so enmeshed in the common folks due to years of mental bondage, oppression, corruption, and cruelty, could not be wiped away even by the presence of their very Savior. Can justification really prevent people from seeing what they in their hearts and minds really want to see? I think so.

Something has to make a person exchange justifications, the food that feeds the habit of mind. Something has to be consumed that is so great in taste and vibrant in color that it makes a small dent in that wall, something that encompasses, as Morgan Freeman said in The Shawshank Redemption "a feeling only a freeman feels." That was the feeling that instilled in his character the willingness to exchange the justifying reasons of keeping parole, the pattern of post-prison to death, in order to grab a passport, and go from bus to plane traversing the Atlantic Ocean in order to see his friend. That something has to transcend the discussion beyond the concepts of right and wrong. It has to inspire change, not instill fabrics of guilt, intimidation, and habitual repetition into how you or I see life.

As I look back at it all, I see that a few of my justified beliefs then were:

1 I had to acquire to believe.

2 I am not accountable for my situation.

3 My friends and family have to agree with me in order for me to believe.

4 If it doesn't feel right, then it must be wrong.

5 If it is uncomfortable, then it is unachievable.

6 I have to see it in order to believe it.

7 If no one I know has done it, then it can't be done.

These were justified beliefs, my proven methods of thought verified by my worldview at the time, a view which came with an instinctual way of digesting information and responding to everything around me. Is it any wonder that, at the time, my habit of mind was adverse to my fulfillment of any goals because they would extend beyond my immediate realm? My fortress was impenetrable; my habits of mind firmly locked in their can't do, can't work tradition.

When I committed to the realization that I wanted something different from my life and to the belief that it could actually happen, I soon came to another conundrum. For me to achieve my desired goal, I would have to exchange one series of justified beliefs for another. Now, the issue wasn't whether the justifications feeding my habit of mind were right or wrong. There was an upgraded question—are my current justifications moving me in the direction of my desired destination and if not am I willing to exchange them? And with that question, the battles begin.

CHAPTER 2

The Seven Battles
in the War

Rarely is war won by one sweeping act of aggression. Wars are won in series of battles, each victorious battle the result of strategy, commitment, and risk. These battles culminate in overall victory, the winning of the war. When Tiger Woods enters the war of a pro-golf tournament, there are many battles with which he must contend, the climate, the competition, the spectators, the critics. In order to win the war, he must successfully prevail in each individual battle.

When a business owner enters the war of business, there are many battles with which that person will have to contend. The economic climate, the customer, the demand, the budget, the competition, and the employees. In order to win the war, the owner must successfully triumph in each individual battle. When a team leader enters the war of teamwork, there are many battles with which that leader will have to contend: the perspective of differing mentalities, the climate, the egos, the challengers, and the critics. In order to win the war, the team leader must successfully overcome each individual battle.

Every war can be translated into a series of battles, each battle distinctive in nature and no doubt requiring a distinctive approach. To win the war, you must be equipped to do three things:

- Identify and select the battles worth pursuing
- Strategize in order to create credible plans
- Equip yourself with the necessary machinery to fight each battle

IDENTIFY AND SELECT BATTLES WORTH PURSUING

Each battle requires an output of valuable resources. Consequently, one fighting a war, such as the war of belief, has to be aware that resources depleted to help win a battle can lead to defeat in the overall war. For this reason, all battles are not worth the fight. Even if one seems in your best interest at the moment of engagement, your agenda should be to fight only those battles imperative to winning the war, not peripheral ones such as winning the acceptance of others, convincing doubters, or a favorable glance from your colleagues.

At the early stages of my conflict with belief, I fought every battle put before me. I battled those who didn't believe by trying to convince them of the correctness of my decisions. I battled the doubters by trying to prove myself in their presence. These battles seemed noble at the time, but as time went on, I found that due to depleted emotional and mental resources, I was unable to give 100% to battles that would directly affect my future. I realized that all battles are not worth fighting. The issue was not ability to win those battles. Instead, the upgraded approach involved deciding whether those battles were worth the resources required to pursue them.

To identify and select battles worth your engagement, always start by asking yourself some important questions. Is the battle directly related to the outcome of the war, in particular, here the war of belief? Will your refusal in engaging in this battle deter you from winning the war? Can you afford the mental and emotional resources that will come from engaging in the battle? Is the battle about the strategy of winning the overall war or is it personal in nature? Remember, to win the war of belief, you cannot use emotional or irrational decision-making in determining whether to pursue battles.

STRATEGIZE TO CREATE A CREDIBLE PLAN

Strategy is simply a method of maneuvering with the intention to reach an objective. Since the objective here is to win the war of belief, all of your strategies have to be designed to reach that target. This requires a commitment on your part to aim only at your objective and to bring your senses into alignment with that goal. This in itself is one of the crucial battles in the war of belief. Since war is traditionally chaotic, keeping focus is imperative in battle due to the emotional and mental debris that comes with engagement. A focused general keeps everyone's eyes on the target and keeps the conversation relevant to the objective, which makes creating strategy plausible.

Great strategy gives birth to credible plans, plans worth fighting for. Such plans are based on more than an emotional impulse; they are derived by looking at all the factors involved in a battle and piecing together a method in which a rational person will believe with both mind and heart. This method is consistent with winning. It is a method built on anticipating plausible scenarios in battle and making plausible plans to overcome them.

EQUIP SELF WITH MACHINERY
TO FIGHT BATTLE

Wars are big budget operations costing in the hundreds of billions, even trillions to run. Fortunately for those of us engaged in the war of belief, the billion-dollar budget is unnecessary. The war of belief is more about the *prioritizing of a budget* than the compiling of a war chest in the billions. Prioritizing a budget simply means devoting necessary resources to places that will help you advance the war. Do you need additional information to help you win the war? If so, are you willing to prioritize your budget to go learn it? The war of belief is not about how much money you have as much it is about where you allocate the funds you have.

JUSTIFIED REASONS TO BELIEVE
OR DISBELIEVE

While engaged in war, we can justify our habit of mind to move in either direction, toward belief or toward disbelief. In this case, belief refers to trusting your habit of mind and the justification that feeds it, and disbelief to mistrusting the habit of mind with the justification that feeds it. When we fight the propensity to move toward a justification that reduces our chances of reaching our goals, the battles will surface. This will help make us victorious in the war of belief.

This process is not about right or wrong, due to the simple fact that both belief and disbelief can be justified. Instead, it is about efficiency. When you target a goal for yourself, you have to ensure your action is bringing you in alignment with the realization of your target. In the following chapters, we are going to look at seven battles necessary to win the war of belief. Each distinctive battle will come with justifications of belief or disbelief, and each battle will be an opportunity for you to engage in and win your war of belief. To target each of these battles one-by-one, you should identify a key battle in which you feel you are engaged at this moment and which you are either focusing your attention, or simultaneously fighting at each warfront.

Keep fresh in your mind that war is not a short-term commitment. War is not pretty, war is not for the faint of heart, and war is not for those unwilling to sacrifice. If you believe success is your true destination, how you fight will show you how much you mean it. The war of belief is not about others; it is a battle in which you voluntarily enroll yourself. I applaud you for your bravery, soldier, and wish you well on your journey.

CHAPTER 3

BATTLE #1

Believing In Your Destination

JUSTIFIED BELIEF	JUSTIFIED DISBELIEF
Ⓐ I SEE OTHERS DO IT	Ⓐ I HAVE LIMITED RESOURCES
Ⓑ I HAVE THE CREATIVITY	Ⓑ I'M LOCKED INTO MY LIFE

Melinda is a successful thirty four-year old executive. Friends and family would never guess that she is soon to enlist to fight the war of belief. She has all the qualities and accomplishments of someone who has already fought this fight: a great career, her own home, and financial growth. When I sat down to interview Melinda, she talked about her college days, her exciting corporate career which includes traveling all over the country, from South America to Asia Pacific. She spoke proudly, and rightly so, of where her hard-work and sacrifice had taken her in her life.

I asked Melinda, if she could give up half of her lifestyle for one thing that is different, what it would be? She radiantly and quickly answered—to be a doctor. Melinda has always had an inherent desire to make an impact on the lives of individuals. She loves medicine, and talks about her dreams of helping low-income children, working in the nonprofit sector and improving heath care. "So why didn't you pursue what you love?" I asked. She explained that while in college, her grades in the sciences where not as impressive compared to other pre-med school majors. For this reason, she switched destinations, to business, in which to her credit she has had much success.

The reason Melinda is enlisting in the war is that she is not fulfilled. Her success in business over the years has yet to silence her longing to make an impact through medicine, or other related means. She wants to do something different, has been wanting to do something different for years, and is very aware she has not been fulfilled despite all her accomplishments to date. Yet with her education, her record of success, and her driven mentality she has yet to pursue her internal yearnings. When I asked her justified reasons for believing she could accomplish her desire to re-enter medical school, she focused on 3 justified beliefs for accomplishing that objective.

- She has seen others accomplish their dreams.
- She believes she has the creativity and discipline to get through med-school.
- She knows that when her mind is made up, she is focused and driven until completion.

When asked about her justified disbeliefs for not pursuing her inner dreams, she again focused on 3 issues:

- She felt she was to old to reenter school again.
- She is locked into her life.
- She believes the risk could backfire on her.

Both conflicting beliefs has kept her stagnant, not in her career and outward success, but where it matters most, in her dreams and inner success. Melinda went on to ask what prevented her for so many years from pursuing what was in her heart? Like many of us, she went for the right and wrong analysis, ready to seek and destroy. We even talked about cost, time, etc. But the issue wasn't skill, resources, self-esteem, or confidence. The issue was destination.

THE SOMETHING THAT TRIGGERS EVERYTHING ELSE

While skill, resources, and ability no doubt play a role in winning the war of belief and accomplishing your goals, the first battle in the war is destination, meaning you must first buy into where you're going. This issue has an effect on whether the other factors needed to win the war will actually surface. The other factors are not going to arrive by only sheer will of thought, but your appetite towards where you are heading will definitely affect what you feed your habit of mind.

To illustrate, a group selects a restaurant to eat, much to the chagrin of one hold-out, who reluctantly agrees only because he is outnumbered. On the way to the destination, the driver finds himself directionless. Which one in the group uses it as a fuse to escalate the situation? Wouldn't this normally be the hold-out? The brief derailment did nothing but agitate the underlying reality that the person wasn't sold on the choice. What comes out of our own mouths or the mouths of others is easiest to grasp because it is perceptible on the surface, so we can spend a lifetime trying to alter how we speak to ourselves, how we need to adjust that self-talk, but seemingly come right back to the same dialogue.

But it is the ignition, the spark that actually supplies the power and directs the angle of response, that needs to be examined. That is the central issue within the concept of destination, that something always triggers everything else. A detective investigating a crime searches for the motive, the trigger, because it uncovers the direction from which the crime sprung. This allows the detective to backtrack along each step, providing a certainty to the implicated perpetrator's guilt.

Many other factors holding the case together may indeed be important, but, facing a shrewd defense attorney, unless holding a signed confession or a videotape catching the perpetrator in the act, without a compelling motive, the prosecutor will have an uphill battle in proving her case. The jury will be interested in what *triggered* the chain of events that led a person to do the unspeakable, what propelled the accused to put his or her fingerprints on such an act.

The trigger is your total appreciation of and conviction in your destination. That doesn't mean you have to understand every facet of the journey in order to buy into the destination. First off, it is impossible to understand every minute detail of a venture. Secondly, circumstances are seldom guaranteed, so mapped out journeys rarely end the way they were choreographed. Third, review the first and second points again. It is highly unlikely that Michael Dell expected to be incorporating his company in 1984, smack in the middle of a full-blown recession. Although faced with the unexpected, he responded as if he had expected it due to the fact he had already bought into the destination.

YOUR TAKE-OFF SETS THE ANGLE OF RESPONSE

In the 1st stage, Melinda's habit of mind was clearly on medschool. In the 2nd stage, on her ascent, she hit unexpected turbulence; her grades didn't measure up. At that stage, her test responses didn't justify a habit of mind leading towards medschool. This justification, when under challenge, was something that was lurking in her for years. *In times of pressure, she admit-*

tedly confirmed her inability to proceed and sought remedies of least resistance, even at the expense of her own dreams.

To believe in your destination, you need conviction more than you need to understand the entire journey in scrupulous detail. Melinda didn't lack the intelligence to create a formula to overcome the change in her circumstance, but she didn't respond confidently and positively to allow those needed factors to come to surface. Buying into your destination involves a burst of solid conviction, trust, confidence, and determination to get to your target. It is the initial take-off, an airplane's crucial short period of runway to air, the couple of seconds that dictates the success rate of the entire trip.

Melinda's issue wasn't intellect, risk, money, or time. All those may be justifiable issues once the goal is airborne. But the challenge, the strong prevailing winds if you will, hit right on the runway, and she had not the thrust or confidence to respond adequately to lift herself above the fray.

A SUCCESSFUL TAKE-OFF CREATES BELIEF CULMINATION

A pilot was asked during an actual Q&A with some college students, if a plane lost all its engines after a commercial airline reached its designated altitude, what would happen? How soon would it take to crash? To the surprise of the group, the pilot highlighted that all was not lost. The plane can glide some considerable distance before a forced landing is administered, after finding some open land. While the group was focused on sudden doom and destruction, the pilot conveyed the options at his disposal for remedying the situation when threatened after a successful take-off.

When your attitude is attached to the certainty of your goal, when you trust in your ability to see it through, your take-off raises you to a place where even under test, you see options and remedies while others crash and burn. This is the power of the successful acceptance of your destination; it triggers the onset of the course leading to the culmination of justified belief, creating a habit of mind that leads you to look for justifications for success even when surrounded by factors that could easily justify disbelief. Culmination does not imply an overnight transformation. It means to reach a climatic point, which happens in stages.

The result would have been different had Melinda taken off with the certainty that her destination was in her hand regardless of the challenges that may surface. It does not mean real issues would not have come to test her journey, but it means that after a successful take-off, like the pilot who, instead of focusing on engine failure to justify a belief that all is lost, she would look at the altitude of her attitude, the power of her hope, examples of her prior successful flights, initiating a response of *what can I do to remedy this situation?* The difference in the question would have culminated in an answer of justified solution, and a reiteration of her justified resolution of belief.

JUSTIFY YOUR SMALL BELIEFS TO
ALTER YOUR BIG DISBELIEF

Constantly justifying your beliefs will alter your concentration on your valid disbeliefs. The reason is that deep inside you want to win the war of belief. We all do, but you will have taken the initial step and put action behind it. The momentum to win is on your side, but momentum sides with thoughts, and if your thoughts are derailed from your justifications in believing in your destination, then a successful take-off is impossible.

In the battle for believing in your destination, you do not need elaborate understanding to win. You need a burst of complete focus on why you can get airborne; you need to avail yourself of the justification for achievement; you need examples of others' successful take-offs; you need to study the beginning not the end of their journey; and you need to compare your mental make-up with theirs at the point of take-off only. That will open the gateway to your understanding that you can have the same take-off success ratio.

Melinda had asserted multiple justified reasons for not believing in her destination. They were valid, but none of them were needed for take-off. Take-off is not about money, availability of long periods of time, or changing one's daily structure. Take-off is about believing that you can simply get airborne. Once airborne, you, like a pilot, will justify reasons to stay in the air. This brings us to the second battle, that some of your reasons will be unbelievable.

CHAPTER 4

Accepting the Fact that
Belief is Unbelievable

JUSTIFIED BELIEF	JUSTIFIED DISBELIEF
Ⓐ I've Seen Others Do It	Ⓐ I Don't See Me That Way Now
Ⓑ Everyone Says I Can Do It	Ⓑ I've Never Experienced Belief

Once you have completed a successful lift-off in a plane and become airborne, you begin to disconnect from everything you tangibly see. You begin to see the buildings, ground, cars, and greenery from a distance as it fades and you duck inside the clouds for a quick peek, emerging into nothing but sun and blue sky. It is truly unbelievable. This battle of the war involves basically the same process, to come to grips with the unbelievable. You can underestimate the process that takes place in the second leading from runway to lift-off; a person literally shifts from walking, what we naturally know and do, to flying, what we don't naturally know or do, and becoming comfortable in that paradox.

The unbelievable belief battle is the struggle to stay grounded while moving from having justifiable beliefs and managing their side effects to unbelievable beliefs and back to justified beliefs again, naturally growing confident as you develop in your understanding of that paradox. Engaged in the war of belief, a successful entrepreneur can shift from being an employee with a great job and security, quit the job to become a laughing stock with no security, build a successful business to return to a state of security, respectability and credibility, and become his or her own boss. In that process, a person usually loses and regains the same things along the way.

Starting a business from scratch, the ex-employee loses belief-affirming factors regardless how great the new project is—the building, the boss, the paycheck, the co-workers, the prepackaged list of duties. This has a powerful effect. The individual is now left with himself or herself. In this situation in the early stages, so many people wonder why they worked so hard for others, more than for themselves, especially if entrepreneurship is something new to them. In this transition, individuals lose visual contact with their affirming beliefs regardless of how much they disliked their job.

As the separation begins, and the externally affirming beliefs disappear, one must accept the paradox of building new tangible belief, generally with very little that is tangible to show for it in the process. In the meanwhile, the individual must remain steady as he or she grows through that process and back to justified beliefs, but this time based on what the person has built in him or herself. Digesting that concept can be truly unbelievable.

SEEING IS NOT NECESSARILY BELIEVING

Remaining steady is more important than comfort. An uncomfortable person who stays unwavering can create success while the opposite is not so true. The separation from affirming beliefs is downright uncomfortable, like a person not used to flying whose steady enough not to scream down the aisles. Being steady involves conviction, while being comfortable means being at ease. There is no ease in piloting your own life.

It is said that seeing is believing. It is not necessarily so in the war of belief; seeing doesn't automatically compute to believing. Believing is an eventuality, meaning as you adjust to the battles and get comfortable with the weapons of choice, you begin to believe in what you see. But in the beginning you have to battle the fact that what you are seeing is usually the direct opposite of what you must believe.

Belief is also defined as truth, the conviction you have in your soul about what is true. This truth becomes your habit of mind. The war of belief simply means battling the terrain to come to a new definition of truth, a new habit of mind. Acquainting oneself only with successful people will not make their habit of mind your truth. It can bring you in contact with individuals who live by a certain code of truth, but your ability to articulate their truth will not make it your truth.

Your truth will become theirs when you see your justification merge with theirs. To illustrate, successful people take risk, and they justify this with the understanding that without risk there can be no reward. You may see them risk and hear them discuss how they risked; yet you stay convinced you can win the war of belief without taking risk. In that event, your truth will not be their truth.

YOU WOULDN'T BELIEVE IT IF YOU TOLD YOU

People in my immediate circle had a hard time comprehending the process of this conflict with belief, the victories, the amazing mental re-shifting, and, of course, the financial opportunities that were emerging for me. However, these things didn't come without sleepless nights, nervous days, and people looking at me peculiarly as I screamed to myself in the car encouraging myself to keep going. I used to get tired of trying to explain and prove it to people. I used to say, "you wouldn't believe it if I told you," and for good reason, because I didn't even believe it when I told myself.

After lift-off I began voraciously taking in everything related to belief, reading the stories of those that had fought the war of belief and came out victorious. Nonetheless, while in the beginning I may have been repeating the quotes, telling the stories, painting the pictures of success to myself, and visualizing victory over the war of belief, I didn't actually believe in what I told myself, not for years. Was I doing something wrong? I was seeing it, talking it, acting it out, but my belief was unbelievable to me at the time.

I get questions from individuals all the time who after lift-off, after taking action to get their dreams airborne and after moving away from those affirming beliefs, question themselves for not believing in their heart what they are actually seeing around them. They see their potential but don't believe it. They see others who are successful, but they don't believe they can do it. They ask what is going on? Am I less deserving? Is it my lack of passion, lack of purpose, or lack of hunger? I say, "Have you ever considered that maybe at this stage you're not supposed to believe in what you see, but that as you propel forward that belief will take its natural course?" Belief means accepting what you believe as truth, specifically here, it means accepting the new justifications you are using to feed your habit of mind.

If a person has been consuming justifications that have burnt justified disbelief in his psyche, simply doing something differently will not make them instantly consumed with belief in what they are now seeing. Remember, the war of belief is battling the terrain to come to your new definition of truth, a new habit of mind. Just as it takes time to form a habit of disbelief, it takes time to form a habit of belief. In the process of war, be willing to look at all areas to ensure you are fighting at full capacity. What you see being at odds with what you believe is not in itself a deal breaker. Remember, as long as what you do is not at odds with what it takes to reach to your target, you will eventually believe it as you see yourself moving closer to your goal.

"That is easier said than done," I would have told myself. Not realizing as I do now that there is a reason I didn't believe then and that the reason has nothing to do with how deserving I am, with what I see, with my conviction, or with my passion. It is all based on something more powerful than all of those: my very survival.

YOUR SURVIVAL IS STRONGER
THAN YOUR BELIEF

"Because beliefs are designed to enhance our ability to survive, they are biologically designed to be strongly resistant to change. To change beliefs, skeptics must address the brain's survival issues." Gregory W. Lester, PhD., a psychologist on the graduate faculty of the University of St. Thomas, Houston, Texas. When I read the professor's well-written essay entitled "Why Bad Beliefs Don't Die," it literally changed the way I looked at belief and indeed led me to agree that seeing does not always mean believing.

Boy, did I need that assurance because at that time I was sitting motionless in the center of the war of belief like a dog caught in a game of "truth or dare" with a cat, frustrated because my arch-nemesis had just completed a loud "meow" and laughed, daring me to say it. Seeing may get compulsive shoppers to the mall, but believing in what we see will target what we hold onto the most strongly, our very survival.

In this war, one has to walk the diligent steps of changing the justified beliefs leading us away from our target of success to the new justified beliefs leading us towards that target. The process of doing so is tedious because it involves blocking that natural habit of mind from returning to those user-friendly survival techniques.

At stages in this journey, I have told myself I couldn't fulfill my dreams while in the midst of fulfilling them. How many times have I told myself I couldn't do it while at the same time actually doing it? Seeing yet not believing, reasoning I must be wrong for having that habit of mind, daily hoping that approach would eradicate it. However, this essay helped me start looking at the crux of my failure to believe what I was seeing. It was the simple fact that I was seeing one thing, yet surviving on the opposite.

EXAMINING YOUR SURVIVAL KIT

Survival is a strong word to connect with belief, especially when you recognize it as a habit of mind preventing you from reaching your target. "You mean I am surviving on justifications that are leading me in the opposite direction of my goals?" I reasoned. That just didn't feel right. Who in his right mind, after volunteering in this war, would then fight in the direction opposite to his goals? However, survival is not about right or wrong, as Dr. Lester explained, "... *the brain doesn't care whether or not the belief matches the data; it cares whether the belief is helpful for survival.*"

And that, my friend, is when the Forth of July took place in the middle of winter, because I heard missiles, firecrackers, gunshots, and my psyche explode all at once. It was life-altering when I understood that, although I was seeing things differently, trusting to the point of believing was still what had helped me survive my entire adult life. It is not what you see, know, observe, or even agree to be true that sparks what you believe, but, more importantly, it is what's in your survival kit.

My kit consisted of seven main tools:

1 Only experts can believe.

2 I am powerless to alter my life.

3 Friends and family have to agree with me in order for me to believe.

4 Any negative reaction is a sign something is wrong.

5 Discomfort means abandon ship.

6 I have to see it in order to believe it.

7 If no one I know has done it, then it can't be done.

I shudder when I think that these weren't just misapplication of thought; these were the beliefs that got me through the days, the weeks, the months, the years. This habit of mind was what I survived on, which, as I look at it now, is the direct opposite of what it takes to win the war of belief to come to success.

I write this for those of you involved in the heavy conflict of the war of belief, wondering whether you are going crazy when you see one thing yet believe another. Can I truly become successful without initially believing in what I am seeing? Is that a conflict that is part of the war? Do you really have to be so consciously sold on it that you can see it unfold from start to finish before your eyes? Some people may quickly develop the propensity to believe in what they see while others may not. Yet the result can still be the same for both; other factors can keep a person afloat in the war as full-blown belief develops.

Mary Kay Ash, the $5,000-investment-to-billionaire cosmetic queen wrote in her autobiography: *"On Friday, September 13, 1963, one month after the death of my husband, Mary Kay Cosmetics opened with myself, nine salespersons, and my twenty-year-old son as financial administrator. How did I know it could do it? Well I didn't! I had no crystal ball. All I knew was **I had to do it**. As far as the predictions of my attorney and accountant, I figured they had no crystal balls either."* Does seeing have to instantly become believing?

When something is so strong that it becomes an obligation to the soul, when words, graphs, statistics, and who agrees doesn't matter and it becomes within you a simple, "I had to do it" or "I have to do it," then you will fulfill it. Your very survival and internal peace will depend on it. You can have that feeling without truly believing. You can stay within that paradox and learn to safely navigate the unbelievable. However, your survival kit will have to be reexamined and more than likely altered, and that will take unbelievable risk.

IT TAKES UNBELIEVABLE RISK
TO ALTER YOUR KIT

In a previous chapter, I wrote the following, *"Keep in mind that, at the moment of research, you are more than likely to sub-consciously be in a bias state, leaning heavily towards justifying your disbeliefs."* In me, that biased state led to natural skepticism toward anything that went contrary to my survival kit.

I was a skeptic towards success, though I wanted it, desired it, and was drawn to its nature. The more I understood the war of belief and the more I recognized what was logical behavior, the more my skepticism caused inactivity. Sometimes I was motionless.

I reviewed my books on success = still couldn't move
I listened to my motivational tapes = still couldn't move
I looked over my personal successes = still couldn't move
I did my daily affirmations = still couldn't move

I knew these things were relevant to my success, relevant to reaching my target. These things that I consciously knew to be in sync with winning the war were the very things that, although seeing, I didn't believe in, to the point that I became angry with the process. Someone saying I was wrong to think that way would have been met with the usual, "Yes, I agree," but that would just reinforce that I was wrong.

Dr. Lester continues, *"[I]n fact, the whole survival value of belief is based on their ability to persist in the face of contradictory evidence."* I existed in contradictions, and the more I persisted in data-gathering about changing myself, the more I felt confused. Data itself doesn't change a person. If data were all I needed, then I could simply have looked in my survival kit, identified how it contrasted with the techniques needed to win the war, and expounded from there. Although that process in itself is necessary to battle, steps need to be taken in the overall war of belief to break the dependency on one's survival kit. In the midst of seeing that I didn't believe, I had to be willing to separate from my kit in order *to* believe.

Dr. Lester continued, "*Thus, trying to change any belief, no matter how small or silly it seems, can produce a ripple effect through the entire system. This is why people are so often driven to defend even small beliefs.*" Connecting with this idea helps one see that attachment to the survival kit is not a right or wrong issue but a survival issue. I've defended my inability to go forward in the face of clear data that it was possible. Crazy isn't it? Or is it?

A ripple effect is just what the war causes. In the process of war, some successful people have had to mentally and emotionally disconnect from the things blocking their target. This can sometimes cause a blowback effect, leading in the interim to families and friends who are not so happy. Very natural things in the survival kit are disrupted by the war, and, failing to address that, I could see clearly and believe nothing. Dr. Lester highlighted three points one needs to take into consideration when attempting to dissuade a person from their beliefs:

1 Don't expect beliefs to change as a result of data, and don't assume one is stupid because his or her beliefs don't change.

2 Address not only the data but also the fundamental implications that changing the related belief will have on the person.

3 Appreciate how hard it is for people to have their beliefs challenged. It is quite literally a threat to their brain's sense of survival.

Seeing can't be believing without coming to grips with and fully understanding the repercussions that seeing while in action will have on the life you now live. Everything changes in combat with belief; you must be willing to risk your survival kit. What is in your kit? What things contradict what you see? Seeing that you can have more, why haven't you trusted and pursued it? Is what connects you to what you dislike about your life more about apparent survival than about your ability to change it? It will take unbelievable risk to change it, but it can be done as you move to the next battle and stop surviving on your current self-brand.

CHAPTER 5

BATTLE #3

Establishing Your
Belief Brand

JUSTIFIED BELIEF	JUSTIFIED DISBELIEF
Ⓐ I Have A Right To Be Great	Ⓐ I Don't Think I'm Smart Enough
Ⓑ I Can Learn How To Make It	Ⓑ I've Made A Lot Of Mistakes

Are you tired yet? I mean, do you really feel it? Do you feel the belief crisis around you? Despite the multiple available sources of information, the web, television, satellite radio, are you feeling a deficiency of belief? Does all the press have to run the exact same headlines—celebrity embarrassing moments, promising politicians, racial conflicts, diet conflicts, national conflicts, mental conflicts? Can't anyone give me something to believe in, I have lamented?

When I began this war of belief some years ago, I used to sit in training classes listening to an instructor tell me what I am not and what I needed to get in order to become what I am not. He didn't get it. I tuned out 95% of his exercise and his positive chanting principles. Others benefitted, I'm sure, but how can I benefit if I am starting with nothing—no foundation, no belief in myself, no reason to chant, no reason to truly believe in believing?

Silently, I sat taking meaningless notes. I could explain what the notes meant, but I had no idea what they meant *to me.* Looking around at the blank faces as we all wrote in unison, I wondered whether the other students were like me, thinking and wanting to stand up and scream at that the top of their lungs, *"Can you please give us something to believe in!!!!!!!?"*

Sitting in restaurants, walking around with the usual crew as we talked about the usual things in the usual settings, in usual tones, receiving the usual answers to the usual questions, ending with the usual emptiness, I silently thirsted for a conversation about something I could believe in. Can we uplift? Can we engage? Can we demand? Can we encourage? Can we stop settling? Can we stop blaming? Can we dig? Can we empower? Can we discover as individuals, come together as a team, and go after something to believe in?

I think back at those moments of desiring more, yet feeling as if that was it, as if where I was would be all I'd go for years to come, recycling the same events, the same conversations, the same justifications, and the same conclusions. We were all belief clones, shaped to form the same conclusions. Regardless of what information was discussed, we clones returned to our survival kit and repeated the same mantra. Our worldview was representative of our conclusions. My worldview was approximately the size of a very small studio apartment, and with that mindset I entered the war of belief.

THE WAR BEGINS RIGHT NOW

You have to adjust to the fact that the war of belief starts now, today, this minute, and that the seconds matter. You must adjust to the understanding that free choice between the ears plays a role in all things and that the first reference point is how we see ourselves. As you navigate the process of belief, information and suggestions on how to win the war will be supplied to you. You will indeed reference yourself, your view, and your thought processes in deciding whether what you hear qualifies as truth or not.

Albert Einstein has been quoted as saying, "If the facts don't fit the theory, change the facts." In the war of belief, we could equate the facts with the individual fighting the war, and the theory with victory and success. You, the individual must be willing to change yourself to align yourself with victory in the war of belief in your life. You must understand that, yes, you do play the most crucial role in the process, not they, but you. When people hear views or suggestions that are clearly important to their victory in the war of belief, most choose not to utilize them and abandon the theory. Very few readjust themselves—the facts. Enlisting in this war is not for the faint of heart, and the tests that come may lead you to seek comfort in the facts as you now live them while instead changing the theory.

Depending on your starting point in the war, that may be an unsettling thought. If you always looked at others first, you will have to get used to understanding that, yes, you matter. If you always had people tell you what to believe and how to believe, you will have to face the fact that you matter. In the war of belief, facing the simple fact that you matter in the process is a process in itself, especially if it is foreign to you like it was to me.

It was foreign to me in the sense that I knew one could become successful but it could not be one like me. I was lacking so much, had so little and would have needed to gain more than I could afford to become free from the invisible bars that were controlling my life. This thought was contrary to the theory of the war of belief. In the war, the individual is a soldier who trusts that he can win and accepts that fact. For me, in the spirit of Einstein, ensuring a successful outcome wasn't about changing the theory but was instead about changing myself.

This part of the process really puts your hands on the controls. It involves taking control by reshaping everything around you, the external, by first reshaping yourself, the internal. While you are not solely responsible for where you are, it is nonetheless you who wants to get out and will have to take solo command of the battle. If others join you, it is fine; if they don't, fine. This is your life, and you can win the war of belief, with or without others. The reshaping process begins with your personal brand.

YOU MUST STAND OUT IN THE AISLE

If you were walking down the aisle of life as if shopping in a store, looking at people as goods you can purchase, and came across yourself, would you pick yourself up off the aisles and head to the cashier for purchase? Before starting with an off-the-cuff, "*of course I would*," take into consideration how you speak to yourself when no one else is around. What is your conversation after a setback or a mistake? If that were all out on display, would you still buy yourself with no refund, no warranty?

I ask because I believe that we are personal "brands." How we display ourselves has a lot to do with our own personal decisions as to whether to buy into the dream we want. Quite frankly, we can fool all the other shoppers in our lives, and have them buy the smile, the confidence, and the convincing looks. But there is one distinguished shopper we can never fool, namely ourselves.

We market things to ourselves everyday. We instinctually and automatically market feelings and outlooks to ourselves. To win the war of belief, you must buy into yourself, which involves saying yes, without hesitation, if offered the opportunity to choose whether to purchase yourself over again. This was what was missing for me in the beginning, when I sat in classes trying to understand how to become what I wanted to become. I couldn't grasp the concept of this external purchase of my dreams due to the simple fact I hadn't the personal wealth to afford what I was asking.

This personal wealth translates into one's attitude and outlook on oneself. My low personal wealth at that time made it impossible for me to conceive of the notion of affording what I wanted in life. Window-shopping involved gazing yet seeing the price as too steep for my existing pedigree, while purchase required having the mental cash to entertain the thought of choosing to walk in my dream or to even hear the deals being offered. Due to the disconnect from window shopping to purchase, the more data I took in regarding winning the war of belief, the more frustrated I became.

In *The Power of Self-Esteem*, Nathan Branden, Ph.D. highlighted the following: *the greater the number of choices and decisions we need to make at a conscious level, the more urgent our self-esteem.* Winning the war of belief no doubt involves your ability to choose; the choices made in the process will reflect your personal brand. That brand places center stage how you see yourself and in turn how you market the value of your product. Increase the value of your personal brand, and you will market the habit of mind needed to afford what that new brand wants to wear in life. However, a brand is not an overnight process. It is born from a concept.

YOUR BRAND IS A CONCEPT, NOT A PRECEPT

When it comes to self-esteem, one can get caught up in precepts, utilizing ideas on how to regulate behavior in order to build self-esteem. No doubt, regulating behavior is a part of the process, but that behavior has to become your own. You have to authenticate real personal esteem to receive real outward change leading toward winning the war. Regulating behavior is not the issue; the issue is the reason the regulating is being done. Plenty of people regulate their behavior to show esteem in front of others. This regulating is done for the others, not for themselves, so in front of people, they are esteemed to the hilt, but when that reason subsides and the people are no longer around, the esteem subsides as well.

Perception may be reality to common folks, but for those enlisting in this war of belief, perception could easily be a fallacy. That's because from a perception standpoint most of us would pass as confident, assertive individuals. But the war will gut you to the core to see whether you can withstand the heat.

When you look at the lives of those who have fought and won the war, from authentic civic leaders like Dr. King and Gandhi, to inventors like the aviation pioneers the Wright Brothers, they show that these people had to put their hearts on the table for all to see. Come criticism, come naysayer, come doubts and come failures, winners of the war had to have the core to contend with the struggles of overcoming odds to win the war. This war is a gut check and shows strength from a perceptional viewpoint. Without a real root in that confidence, a person can get chewed up on the runway.

Instead of beginning with a precept, meaning your first point of reference on how you should act to ensure optimal esteem, begin with a concept. Keep in mind that most of our esteem has been given to us. While the precepts may have been correct or even invaluable, most information on self-esteem is on point. Our angle of concentration is not the information, but our ability to link ourselves to it. We are not interested only in the external reality, which can lose its luster under severe test. We want our esteem to be an innate part of our being, not only what we show, but what we *are* which by extension shows.

A brand begins with a concept, the creator usually sitting down and brain-storming general ideas regarding the shape, look, and feel of the product. She may think about cost, how the market will respond to it, and what value will she place on it. All of these steps are essential to cultivating the best brand for success. For marketers to get on board and create winning campaigns, they must buy into an exciting brand.

Creating your personal brand is no different. It first involves a brainstorming session with yourself, identifying what is needed from an internal imaging point of view so as to create a brand. When reference has you responding instinctually towards justified beliefs, that brand will serve as your personal compass and show itself by how you react to the steps needed to get to the end-zone of your professed goals.

You can create your brand right now. It is free of charge. You just need to look realistically at your target for success and to start by answering a couple of questions:

- What type of attitude is associated with a person who has accomplished his or her dreams?
- How would that person react to setbacks, failures, and criticism?

- What would that winner learn from winning and losing in order to keep heading towards his or her target?
- When you see a winner, what does he or she look like, and when you hear a winner speak, what does it sound like?

After you answer these questions, cross-reference with your internal disposition. How do you measure up? What image touch-up would you make? What brand of yourself do you see formulating? Remember, you are creating a brand. Don't concentrate on what you are not; just be free and create that brand. To solidify your core internal image, answer these following questions:

- What will your attitude be for winning the war of belief?
- How will you respond to setbacks or failures?
- How will you learn from wins and losses to get to your target?
- While engaged in the war, what will people see when they notice you coming and hear you speaking?

You have just created your concept, your brand. Just filter all your decision-making through this concept, and your perception will soon become real. How you see things will change. How you hear things will be altered, providing the needed components to assist you in fighting the war of belief.

Once your brand is established, it will be time to create a powerful marketing campaign, one that is directly related to the next battle, your belief maze.

CHAPTER 6

BATTLE #4

Expanding your Belief Maze

JUSTIFIED BELIEF	JUSTIFIED DISBELIEF
Ⓐ I'm My Own Person	Ⓐ But That's All I Know
Ⓑ I Can Make Own Decisions	Ⓑ What If Others Don't Agree?

One morning, in the midst of a grueling battle with confidence and still fully in engaged in the war of belief, I reflected on the setbacks, failures and disappointments in my life. Of course, that reflection involved doubt, fear, and uncertainty which usually accompany the process of selling oneself the brand of lack of confidence.

I had a speaking engagement that morning, so I awoke pretty early to ensure my commute wouldn't be hampered by the traffic on the freeway. While I got dressed, that battle with confidence, an integral part of the war of belief, that had me mentally questioning, can I really do this? Can I really win this war of belief and arrive at my destination? I carried these questions with me as I grabbed my briefcase and got into the car. Can I really win this war? Is it truly possible?

To get to the nearest highway, I had to travel over a steep mountain leading towards the interstate entrance. Here I was heading up this mountain, still asking myself if winning this war of belief truly possible for me? I kept repeating this thought until it rolled out of my mouth out-loud, but just as the last word of my question filled the car, I had reached the top of the mountain.

It was a breathtaking scene. The sun had just risen, with its bright yellow lights ducking behind the trees, peeking out gently just enough to show the splendor of its contrasting yet brilliant merging colors. The sky was radiant blue with a sprinkling of white clouds hanging like diamond earrings accessorizing its perfectly assembled outfit, and a few birds flew past looking like the last stroke on the just-completed masterpiece painted by the brush of a smiling Picasso. At that moment, I asked and heard the question again: . . . *Julius, can you really win this war?*

One of the tales of my childhood involves my mother relating to me that after the Creator had finished the making of the first human, the angels applauded at the brilliance of its majesty. As a kid, I couldn't fully comprehend the notion that angels who have the power to play superman would applaud me, a boy who didn't have the wit to get through the second level of Pac-Man.

Yet at the top of the hill, while in awe of the scene, I thought to myself, "Here I am, breathless at the beauty of the sun, and yet I am asking the designer of this inanimate object, the very one who designed me, whether I can really win this war." Why was I asking "can I"? Was "can I?" truly the issue? Can I, after peeking under the hood of the magnificence of the human design, justify a failure to win this war as due to a lack of some kind? No, I could not, certainly not on the premise of pure capability.

So I reasoned that "Can I win?" couldn't be the correct question. The question was not, "Can I win the war?" Instead the question was and is, "Can my current habit of mind digest the reality of victory in the war of belief?" In essence, "Can I adjust to the fact that the war has been won, not by my personal exertion, but by my personal existence?" Simply put, victory doesn't lie in the strategy of deciding what you want to become, but instead lies in what you believe about the person forming the strategy. If a person does not see himself or herself as victorious, how can that same person create a strategy of victory?

YOU CAN LIVE IN VICTORY RIGHT NOW

Victory is yours. This war of belief has already been won by you. Right this very second, the victory of the war is yours to claim, what would you do? Would you start looking around and taking visual inventory of what you've accumulated up to this point in life? Would you start mentally adding up your wins and losses in life and trying to justify that declaration to yourself? Would you ask yourself what you have done to claim victory? Or would you instead say "Yes," affirming your right to be victorious in the war of belief? And would you live by that declaration, hear by that declaration and see based on that declaration that victory is already yours?

I was facilitating a discussion with a panel of highly successful individuals who had already won the war of belief in their own lives. About one hundred individuals, still heavily involved in the conflict of making their own dreams a reality, were asking them questions. One common thread in their questions to these victors surrounded the need to find out the strategy, the day-to-day of what they did externally. They sought to compare notes regarding strategy, what to do, how many phone calls to make, how many customers to target, and how many books to read.

Yet what didn't get asked was what these victors' habits of mind. No one asked about their mentality. Their way of reasoning was lost in the mire of seeking the external details of their battles. The strategies of those who have won the war of belief are legendary, from Larry Page and Sergey Brin, the founders of Google, to Oprah Winfrey. Those include what they did day by day to win the war of belief. But what about the mindset, the thinking process that went into the development of their strategies? The truth is that the factor that led to their victory was not the particular external strategy they utilized, but was instead the audacious proclamation of victory prior to the development of the external strategy and the living by that proclamation.

I do not intend to minimize strategy and its role in the war of belief, but instead to maximize the understanding of your mentality as the marketing you will use to advertise to yourself, hence affecting the very way you compose strategy. So many individuals are hesitant when invited to fight the war of belief, while concentrating on issues such as money, time, commitment, and the length of dedication to the battle. While these factors are relevant, those who have declared victory over their war of belief and lived by that declaration, have by doing so brought themselves much closer to victory than by the questions they asked regarding strategy. When questions about money, time, and commitment rolled from their tongue, it was only in the framework of winning, instead of the framework of itemizing whether they can win. Can you tell the difference?

A person seeking to itemize whether he or she can win is looking to see if he or she has enough money, time, and resources to even begin fighting the war, while the person questioning from a victorious mind is asking about those same concerns in order to see what else is needed to ensure victory is reached. One is going for a target already designated, while the other is deciding whether he or she has what is necessary to even create a target. It is the direction of the strategy, not the strategy itself that creates the victory.

Do you think it was the strategy that ensured Walt Disney victory, the particular way he responded to rejection, setbacks or naysayers? Was it strategy that catapulted Chanel founder CoCo Chanel from her mother's death at six-years-old to abandonment on the streets of France by her Father, to orphanage, to the luxury brand we know today? Strategy is nothing more than methods, but a winning strategy is the by-product of a victorious mind.

What one must realize when reflecting on the stories of those that have won the war of belief is that their strategy was guaranteed to work due to the significant fact that they had already claimed victory and lived and breathed that brand of thought. This is not a cliché: "If you build it, they will come." It involves a victorious habit of mind that will keep you building and adding new attractive features, until they come. It is the last person standing that wins the war, and how long you stand is linked to the foundation on which you are standing. A habit of mind of claiming victory over the war will keep you steady through the unpredictability of combat. An undetermined mind will stand on any foundation since its own is not determined. Once again, I ask can you take in the fact that you are victorious now and live by that proclamation.

WHAT WAS YOUR BELIEF INHERITANCE

Tracey, a mother of two young boys, wanted for years to make a move from her career in corporate America to fulfilling the dream of venturing into her own business, yet due to fear, she repeatedly put it off. After dwelling in that fear for some time, she finally got the gumption to go out on a limb and do it. I caught up with her a few years into her venture, still fresh in the early battle stages of developing a profitable business. When I interviewed her, I asked her what the greatest impact was that led her to move forward in pursuing her dreams and entering the war of belief.

Becoming choked up, she told me about her young son who for years wanted to take up karate but that she refused to allow it due to a fear that he would get hurt (which was in itself a justified belief). However, when she ventured out to conquer her own fears, she simultaneously had a change of heart and allowed her son to begin karate. He became great at it, with the trophies to prove it. She shuddered to think what precedent would she had created in his life had she held him back from learning that winning comes with sacrifices, risk, and at times pain, and how many things she would have denied him in her fear of seeing him hurt.

How did Tracey exchange one set of justified beliefs, which prevented her from allowing her son to take up karate for another set of justified beliefs of allowing him to enter competition under the same circumstances? She loved her son, no doubt, but her belief in him was connected to her belief in herself. Her definitions of fear became his as well. Once she ventured beyond the habits of her mind, she granted her son his wish to venture out as well. Love may be something we have felt and were given by our parents, but few of us felt that we were believed in enough to claim victory right now over the war of belief.

This is not an issue of right or wrong. Nor is it an issue of whether our parents loved us or not. This is an issue of habit of mind, and regardless of how our parents loved us they could only give us what they themselves had grown accustomed to. Parents instinctively tell their kids they can do whatever their heart's desire. However, as that child grows and its parents prepare the child for the real world, that real world is really their world. As loving parents, they helped their child to the best of their ability. Regardless of intent, desire and motive, a parent ordinarily gives the child what the parent himself or herself has or had. Most of our parents gave us their belief as an inheritance, which for the most part didn't coincide with a foundation of victory over the war of belief.

Your belief inheritance has to be addressed in a non-judgmental and non-resentful way. We all inherit a deck of cards with which we have to play life, some cards were bad hands. Maybe I am naïve to believe that if given the choice, people would give their kids the right hands to play with. Some are victims of such a bad deck that, emotionally speaking, folding is a viable option.

To change this, someone has to look at the hand he or she has been dealt and courageously yell for a new card dealer. Someone has to bring positive power and optimism to the table. Someone has to take it upon himself or herself to change the hand for the rest of a family that may be too emotionally tired to play due to a legacy of losses and folding hands bad enough to justify not even playing anymore. That someone may be you. However, when asked whether you can declare victory right now, your belief inheritance will dictate your answer.

Claiming victory means recognizing you have the right to put a strangle-hold on your dreams and not let go regardless of how circumstances, feelings of inadequacy, failures, and setbacks try to pry you away. You may ask how you can possibly claim victory with these seemingly negative conflicting thoughts swirling around while fighting the war of belief. How can questioning oneself lead to unquestionable victory?

If the access to instant information has not taught us anything else, it has certainly cleared up the notion that perfection exists in any segment of the world. We are all flawed, but after claiming victory to a desired dream, individuals can display perfection in certain segments, seconds, minutes, and hours of the day. Those moments of perfection, although minuscule compared to their times of imperfection, have created a bountiful thought process which leads to the unfolding of a life of abundance.

You declare victory now because your declaration is not based on what you feel you are, but on what you are capable of feeling you are. You will be in tune after due process with this battle. What this battle breaks though is the most significant part of the journey, your own self-declaration, which is connected to your habit of mind. James Allen so clearly highlighted this in his 1902 classic release *As a Man Thinketh*, in which he wrote, *"Every man is where he is by the law of his being; the thoughts which he built into his character have brought him there and in the arrangement of his life there is no element of chance."*

Connect that thought with the finding from the renowned ThinkQuest Foundation simply comparing a computer to the human mind as follows: *"1999's fastest PC processor chip on the market was a 700 MHz Pentium that did 4200 MIPS. By simple calculation, we can see that we would need at least 24,000 of these processors in a system to match up to the total speed of the brain! Meaning the brain is like a 168,000 MHz Pentium computer.*" In 2000, AMD claimed they had the fastest chip which was 850MHz. You get the point; you claim victory by being alive. You feel victory by entering the right software for your mind to lead you to your target.

Repairing mental "software" is not about going backwards to find out who hacked your system in the first place, but about starting your data entry right now, identifying and understanding what you need put in the mind in order to stop lifelong glitches and viruses that have built up to the point that you've been living a life of predestined thought, predestined action and predestined conclusions.

This new data entry done successfully will introduce you to a new you, helping you claim victory now, instantly adjusting the belief inheritance in your favor. Reprogramming is a must, which involves weaving old habits of mind with new habits without crashing the system due to the side-effects that come with the process. A maze is not easy to expand, but it must be done to digest the victory awaiting you in your war of belief.

DO YOU KNOW WHY YOU'RE RUNNING IN THE MAZE?

If you kept a group of mice running in a maze for years, daily moving in the same directions as the walls of the maze dictate, then suddenly after years of such endless repetition and rigid continuity you pulled up the maze right in the midst of their daily routine, what do you think would be the reaction of the mice? Would they run the maze on memory alone or would they start running in circles? Probably both, but we can be certain about one thing, they wouldn't suddenly start running straight for the exit to their freedom.

That maze will have made its imprint and when the walls are lifted, the mice will find themselves not knowing in which direction to run anymore. They will have to detox from running in a prescribed maze in order not only to see the exit but to trust that it is truly representative of their freedom after running in the direction of perceived right for such a long period of time.

Expanding your belief maze starts when you stop running the rehearsed maze you have unintentionally inherited and start charting your own way, designing your own maze to lead you directly to your target. In doing so, you must successfully handle the side effects that come with lifting the walls, to which you've grown so accustomed, and start retreading new walls leading to new action.

So, can you declare victory in the war of belief right now? Can you comfortably say you own it? Saying "Yes" freely and feeling it is your first recognition of the exit that will lead to the beginning of reprogramming your habit of mind so that you can market to yourself what is needed to win. If a person cannot say, "Yes" to a declaration of victory, he or she leaves himself or herself open to justifying non-victory, soon to settle for defeat. A person who settles does not always knowingly choose to do so, but unknowingly has to because in the mall of success the product called "indecision" sits on the same shelf as the product called "no." Both brands are marketing to the buyer as defeat.

So, can you say "Yes" affirmatively? If you cannot, it may have to do with how the walls of your maze have been built. How we react to the very notion of crossing belief barriers comes from our belief inheritance. One cannot underestimate the walls of the maze. They've been fortified heavily withstanding the blows of many individuals that have run into them. They are fortified to the point that even after the wall is removed, the individuals automatically stay on course running the now invisible maze.

The run is subconscious. Prior to declaring a new target, I was just subconsciously heading in the same maze prescribed to the runners before me. No one questions the wall because it is so well fortified, so logical to our reasoning, so right in our view. When I realized that it was time to chart out a new maze, I soon came to grips with a mind-blowing realization. The biggest ingredients keeping me running in lockstep weren't right, logical, or reasonable. To the contrary, it was unintentional pessimism.

UNINTENTIONAL PESSIMISM KEEPS YOU IN THE MAZE

Have you ever told people about your great dreams and ambitions, and before they even ask you serious questions about your venture, they give you all the reasons it won't work? Welcome to unintentional pessimism. Have you ever watched the news and the only things they tell you are those that leave you feeling hopeless and restless? Yes, that's unintentional pessimism.

Have you ever simultaneously told someone how great and terrible your day was in the same breath at the same time? Yep, that's unintentional pessimism. Have you ever held a staff meeting focused on inspiring the team, yet someone on the team who swears he or she is on board brings up all the reasons the team is uninspired? Yes, my friend, you've been a victim of unintentional pessimism.

"A pessimist sees the difficulty in every opportunity; an optimist sees the opportunity in every difficulty." —William Churchill. A pessimist has an inclination to emphasize adverse conditions and possibilities or to expect the worst possible outcome, while the optimist has an inclination to place the most favorable construction upon actions and events or to anticipate the best possible outcome.

Unintentional pessimism is what fortifies the walls of the maze. It prevents you from declaring victory in the war of belief, and it keeps some so emotionally reactive that they are unable to form a clear positive understanding of the power of who they are due to the pessimism. This is not always done intentionally, but for the most part unintentionally.

Intentional pessimism was legitimately used to warn us as kids when things were dangerous, such as crossing the street, playing with strangers, disobeying the law, playing with matches, etc. These were things our parents knew would lead to harm, so they rightly emphasized the adverse consequences of heading in those directions, using a "pessimistic" outlook. The fear of getting hurt coupled with fear of reprisal for disobeying the folks, kept most of us at bay.

Safety was the name of the game and loving parents intentionally did their part to keep us safe in the real world. However, what happened when their real world conflicted with our real world? When their proven safe dreams, aspirations, and understanding of the real world conflicted with our unproven dreams, aspirations and goals, didn't they warn us from straying due to fear of us getting hurt, and didn't they do it to keep us safe and with every good intention? Just like Tracey, whom I mentioned earlier, who lovingly did so with her son, didn't our parents emphasize the adverse consequences of heading in those directions as well? That great intentional endeavor may have lead to unintentional pessimism.

*25-year-old Mike had ambitions to travel the world. His father, when thinking of his son's safety, said, "No. It's **dangerous**; he needs to work with a good company, with a good **safety net**." Mike's father has never traveled outside the U.S. himself due to the same fears.*

*52-year-old Sara has been in the car business for over 20 years, but she has a passion for photography and is known in the community for her excellent photos. Yet when she talks about her dream of traveling and pursuing this career she loves, in the same breath, she talks about her **fear** of making no paycheck and her **anxiety** over taking the **risk**.*

*24-year-old Heather was thinking about moving out of the rural town in which she grew up, but her parents warned her of the **risk** associated with being a single girl living in a **dangerous** city. Her parents had met in this town, married in this town, and planned to retire in the same town.*

*Grant and Leo had a great idea for a business, but when they shared the idea with their friends, they were **warned** and **cautioned** about the statistics having to do with small businesses and their **failure ratio.***

All of these are examples of unintentional pessimism. When people share their goals and receive sincere feedback that unintentionally emphasizes the adverse consequences of heading in those directions.

Attempts to go beyond the wall of the maze can invoke feelings of guilt, anxiety, fear, and uncertainty. I remember when I told my mother what I was pursuing. In her kind unintentional way, she gave me every reason why I needed to be careful. Safety was the name of the game, and, in the game of safety, pointing out every plausible danger was not just standard, but necessary.

Expansion is not a result. It is a beginning. It is not the finality of creating your wall. It is the initial step. It is being resolute in seeking a solution. The wall forms your boundaries, and those need to be fortified properly to withstand the pressure that accompanies combat.

When one is seeking to accomplish a goal, he or she needs tunnel vision. In the tunnel, you see the mental leaning that creates the strategy you establish for yourself to secure victory. This mental leaning is nothing more than a fraction of a thought. Yet, in that brief moment in time, wars of belief are won and lost.

It does not take long for unintentional pessimism to be injected into a person's psyche, but the damage can last a lifetime. How long does it really take for a well-intended person to tell someone, "You can't do that"? How long did it take for you to read it? Didn't catch it? Let's try it again, simply say, "You can't do that." How long did it take? A half a second. Yet put that between the ears of an unsuspecting person with the goal of winning the war of belief for a couple of minutes throughout the day, and you can navigate that person's decisions. Five minutes of hearing what you cannot do will do its job in determining what you will do.

Victory is yours. This war of belief has already been won by you. Right this very second, the victory in the war is yours to claim. What would you do at this point? Would you start looking around and taking visual inventory of what you've accumulated in life? Would you begin mentally adding up your wins and losses in life trying to justify that declaration to yourself? Would you ask what you have done to claim victory? Or would you say, "Yes," affirming your right to be victorious in the war of belief?

Unintentional pessimists do so much damage due to the simple fact that we believe they are credible in our lives. We openly lean them an ear. More than likely, they are our trusted advisors. That is the power of the wall which guards the maze.

Rarely are people trapped in mediocre mazes built by strangers. The felon holding folks hostage is frequently someone we've invited into our lives, with whom we talk daily, socialize frequently and have a trusting relationship. He or she usually presents unintentional pessimism, which needs to be nullified with intentional optimism.

INTENTIONAL OPTIMISM STARTS THE REDESIGNING

Optimism is not naiveté. It's not blindly jumping for joy about things that have no credible foundation. Optimism is not separate from reality. It involves looking at reality and seeing the opportunity that lies within. Optimism is an inclination to put the most favorable construction upon actions and events or to anticipate the best possible outcome.

Optimism is not related to having all the answers. It is not about being able to peer inside a crystal ball or be the most jovial in the room. Optimism hedges on two factors: positive construction and positive anticipation.

Positive Construction

Positive construction simply means finding the elements within circumstances to construct an optimistic outlook on things. This doesn't mean a person builds with the intent to overlook the clear and present challenges that sit before them. As mentioned, optimism is not a state of naiveté. It is not even the answer. It is the intent behind finding the answer, solving the problem, overcoming the challenge. One of Webster's definitions for intent is, "the state of mind in which an act is done." Thus, an optimist's mind is inclined to see the most favorable elements of a situation.

Positive Anticipation

Anticipation is a prior act. It is the pre-conclusion that we give any situation prior to its actually ending. Positive anticipation involves seeing whatever situation is at hand end favorably for you, and walking and breathing from that that angle. Positive anticipation means taking control of your thoughts, refusing to allow dire messages about the circumstances to subconsciously dictate your pre-conclusion, to prevent forecasting your own ending, and instead to take control of your thoughts and act according to your self-prophecy.

To most individuals, an optimist may seem like a fish out of water. At times of crisis, the optimist will point out things on which to build, while the crowd will tear things down. This reaction by the optimist is not automatic. While some of us are predisposed to seeing the glass as half-filled, keeping that predisposition requires intent. The difference between the optimist and the pessimist is based on what each pulls from circumstances to construct his or her thoughts. The optimist neither changes nor overlooks the situation. The optimist's view just provides him or her with more of an opening to resolve it. With intentional optimism, a person can see the same things, yet provide him or herself with a way to resolve them. Let's review once again those examples of the unintentional pessimist, but this time we will include an intentional optimistic response by the listener.

*25-year-old Mike had ambitions to join a new and exciting company which would give him the chance to travel the world. His father, thinking of his son's safety, said, "No. It's **dangerous**, he needs to work with a good company, with a good **safety net**." Mike's father has never traveled outside the U.S. himself due to the same fears.*

Mike's response: *You know, you're correct. Safety is always a concern, but millions of people do it every year, pops. There are **clear guidelines** on how to **stay safe** while traveling abroad. Also, the company has already sent over a few folks, and **everything worked out**.*

*52-year-old Sara has been in the car business for over 20 years, but she has a passion for photography and is known in the community for her excellent photos. Yet when she talks about her dream of traveling and pursuing this career she loves, in the same breath, she talks about her **fear** of making no paycheck and her **anxiety** over taking the **risk**.*

Sara's response: *Before I draw my conclusions, let me see whether there are **examples of success**. Maybe I can start part-time right now for just a **few hours** a week, which will cost hardly anything. Maybe, I can get some clients around here to start.*

*24-year-old Heather was thinking about moving out of the rural town in which she grew up, but her parents warned her of the **risk** associated with being a single girl living in a **dangerous*** *city. Her parents met in this town, married in this town, and planned to retire in the same town.*

Heather's response: *I've done some **research**, and it's not as dangerous as you think. You know, Chelsea's parents were just as concerned, but after visiting her, they were relieved. Granted, some parts have safety issues but **I'm looking at another location where safety is hardly an issue.***

*Grant and Leo had a great idea for a business, but when they shared the idea with their friends, they were **warned** and **cautioned** about the statistics having to do with small businesses and their **failure ratio.***

Grant's and Leo's Response: *No one has touched on **examples of Walt Disney and other business successes**. Don't you guys work for big businesses that began as small businesses? The risks are no doubt there, but the **ways to overcome** them are there as well.*

The difference between the optimist and pessimist is based on what the person pulls from circumstances in constructing his or her thoughts. Optimism neither changes nor overlooks a situation. It just provides a person with more of an opening to solve the issues that have been put before him or her. With that resolve to be intentionally optimistic, let's move on to the next battle, understanding the game within belief.

CHAPTER 7

BATTLE #5

Understanding the Game Within Belief

JUSTIFIED BELIEF	JUSTIFIED DISBELIEF
(A) I Can Learn How To Adapt	(A) But My Schedule Is Hectic
(B) I Can Make The Decision	(B) But They Don't Agree With Me

There exists a game within belief. A game is defined in the dictionary as nothing more than a procedure or strategy for gaining an end, the end to your goal. That goal is winning the war of belief in your life. The game is formulated around your objective, and thus involves procedures necessary to create the habit of mind to ensure that your goal materializes.

Look at the game within belief as dependent on your mindset, which is imperative to how you play. How you play will be discussed in the final battles 6 and 7 of the next chapter. The game within belief is based on your mental posture which is imperative in the war of belief. There are plenty of individuals with the talent to totally annihilate the war of belief, yet due to incorrect set-up or mental posture they cannot even see their own talent. The game within belief is based on three vital components that you must understand to play the game effectively and efficiently:

- **Access**
- **Authorization**
- **Application**

We will discuss all three components and see how they relate to the game within belief, which sets the boundaries of ensuring your talents are gauged correctly to win the war of belief.

Access

Whatever you want in life involves access. To simply get to the corner market, you'll need access to transportation or access to the will to get up and take a stroll to the corner. Nothing happens without involving access, the freedom or ability to obtain or make use of something. The key word in that meaning is "freedom," the precious yet rarely obtained jewel of life.

To have freedom, you must become the authority on what you want. You have to become the CEO of your life. If you want the freedom of self-esteem, then you need to ensure your esteem hedges on you, that you can have access to that feeling. If you want financial freedom, then you need to have access to that process, have the skills to earn that freedom salary or be the person granting you access to pay yourself on a freedom scale. You want spiritual freedom? Then, you had best have access to the giver of that freedom, access to study and navigate in the way the authentic freedom-holder intended. Without access to the door that opens to your dreams, your belief will not materialize, regardless of how well-intended you are and regardless of your talent.

"Access to what," you may ask? The answer is—access to the emotional and mental freedom needed to form the habit of mind necessary for you to reach your target. At first blush, you may reason that of course you have access to create your own habit of mind. This is not necessarily so. It all depends on your belief inheritance. Most of us didn't inherit access to the dreams we wanted, access to believing they could surface in our on lives.

We live in a culture that plants dependency and promotes a strategy that makes it grow, whether it is financial dependency, "Shop to you drop;" spiritual dependency, "Follow me I have the answer;" or mental and emotional dependency, "You need these exteriors to feel good about yourself." Where limited access breeds, people will have a lockstep reaction to anything that contrasts with the culture of their dependency, and freedom will never be attained.

Those that have won the war of belief had to gain much more than limited access. They became disenchanted with limited access and wanted full access to the source. They are the ones researching the car value prior to walking inside the dealership, and, while the majority of buyers are fascinated by emotionally stimulating sales banners and sales talk, they start the negotiation with the invoice price or the actual price at which the dealership bought the car itself.

You want financial freedom? You'll need to have access to the source who writes the check or become the source yourself. You want spiritual freedom? You'll need access to the source creating what you believe. You want mental and emotional freedom? You'll need access to the source navigating how you feel or better yet become that source yourself. But access is not free. You'll need to understand the second component in the game, authorization.

Authorization

Access can only be sought from and granted by someone having authority, and depending on your belief inheritance this could be a scary thing to face. Do you have authority to gain access to the means to your goals? When I spelled out my goals, I had no idea at the time that I would soon awaken to the rude realization that I never had authority to grant access to what I wanted in life.

Talent means nothing if fear and guilt has control over your decision to grant access to use those talents. The pursuit of self-esteem is meaningless if you want to please everyone. Then, your authority is them-esteem, and regardless of what you want for yourself the access to getting it is based on them. Spiritual freedom is counterfeit if it means following the ideologies of others and not the source from which it streams, and financial freedom cannot be captured if you are enslaved to your daily complaints.

You have to be willing shake things up and cease being dependent and subservient. You have to become the authority who grants your self-access to what you want in your life. I have been called every name in the book due to my shake-up, including prideful and stubborn. I've been told I would never accomplish it. I was told I was an embarrassment for what I gave up to get my authority. The shake up hurts. It is a gut check of a different kind. Nonetheless, I got my authority as did others before me, and access soon followed. I look back at people who didn't stand up for their authority, and they are still in line waiting on someone to grant them access. History has made perfectly clear that will never happen.

Application

Everything you learn in this game within belief means nothing until you seal it with the last component—application. Application does not only mean putting something to use. It's how you put it to use. It's the strength behind the action. It's playing the game with full authority and being resolute about obtaining access. It's about having the correct mental posture, power, resolve, and resilience when executing the game plane. While doing so, you have to take note of the characteristics of the game of belief, which create the boundaries in which to play.

BELIEF IS NOT A GAME ABOUT YESTERDAY

The past is irrelevant to greatness, so it is also irrelevant to the game of belief. Just ask Robert Johnson, Walt Disney, Bill Clinton, Oprah Winfrey, Michael Dell, Anna Roddick, and Larry Ellison. Ask them if they allowed their lives to be determined by their yesterdays.

How about you? Your belief should be dictated by what you do today and the days hereafter. Your past does not negate your right to succeed in this game. Neither does it care where you come from, what people say about you, what mistakes you have made, nor even how you feel about yourself. The game is focused on your inner potential, which still remains despite the past.

BELIEF IS NOT A SHORT-TERM GAME

This game is not short-term. Yet most people may play it for a minute and, as soon as it becomes uncomfortable, cut the game off and return to their original way of life. This crash-and-burn syndrome begins with a person's inability to recognize from the start that the game will demand compromise on many levels.

Let's be realistic. If a person has been working in a job he or she dislikes or is not making the money he or she likes, this person has minimally grown accustomed to the game he or she is already playing. When the going gets tough in the war, returning to the game with which that person is most familiar is not difficult at all.

One may be amazed that the naysayers didn't listen to great opportunities as did innovators such as Martha Stewart and Michael Dell. The innovators didn't believe in returning to the game of the status quo. They defined the game in such a way as to complete the war of belief, realizing it is not a short-term process.

BELIEF IS NOT A GAME DICTATED BY EMOTIONS

Belief has characteristics resembling reality. It cannot be emotional because its system is based on facts. Those involved in the game of belief tend to be realistic about the war as well. Some, however, mistakenly believe that the game will cater to their emotions, misinterpreting the war as a game of compromise and renegotiation.

Since the game exists on facts, emotions cannot be the controlling factors in choosing what plays you need to move forward. In the war of belief, your game strategy cannot be created based on how you feel but must instead be based on what is real.

The game of belief will not slow down because you can't keep up. Belief will not take it easy because you want it easy. Belief is never going to lower its standards for you based on how you feel about yourself. Belief is a progressive entity always moving forward, creating power activities for those willing to accept their inner potential.

The game of belief approaches you as if you are already a commodity. It will not listen to your excuses and negative self-talk about what you can't do. The game of belief has had winning participants who were high school and college dropouts, single moms, those with learning difficulties, those who suffered severe abuse, and those in financial ruin. All of those people have been victors in the war, despite their circumstances and shortcomings. They were willing to come up to the game's standards, so don't expect the game to ask anything less from you.

BELIEF IS NOT A GAME FOR THE INFATUATED

Initially, I believe everyone marveled when introduced to the results of belief, because of its appeal, how it looks, and even how good it feels. This is what I refer to as the infatuation stage, and it sustains people for short-time. However, initial meetings with the game of belief and the sudden attraction when in the game, will not sustain you through the turbulence of the war.

Most Hollywood movies present their stories of belief in an infatuation style, the rags-to-quick riches, and the instant sight to instant love happily ever after. The only factual thing in that Hollywood screenplay is the time that infatuation lasts—approximately 90 minutes. Infatuation is not a sustainable quality in the game and especially not in winning.

Many people have had great ideas that you have never heard about. Many people you have never heard about have initially come in contact with the game of belief. Why? This is because the initial meeting with the game, the sudden attraction to the possibility of being involved with it based on what it can do for you, will not sustain you during the rough times in your growth.

In a relationship, the investigation into a person's positive predominant qualities that you spend years getting to know is what makes the relationship solid, even when the storm seems to hover over it at times. Infatuation is not a sustainable quality in any relationship, and it is equally not so with belief. Those in the game based only on infatuation have no actual facts to sustain them when challenges arise, when opposition arises from their patterns of thought or from the questioning of those around them. Since we have explored the battles and familiarized you with the needed components of the game, we are going to approach the final battles to compile all this together, which informs thinking like a coach and playing like an athlete.

CHAPTER 8

BATTLES #6 AND #7

Believing Like a Coach & Playing Belief Like an Athlete

JUSTIFIED BELIEF	JUSTIFIED DISBELIEF
ⓐ I Know Positive Thoughts Create Positive Results	ⓐ Losing Creates Internal Havoc
ⓑ Show me the Rules I can Play the Game	ⓑ Being the Leader is Scary

We all run on the treadmill of life. However, something in the past, whether it was local or world news, individual growth or change of events, may have forced you to reevaluate where you are and where you are going and put into question whether you're heading in the direction of your dreams. At that moment, you probably looked and told yourself that you needed to change, needed to redirect your energy to the goals you wanted in your life. But years later after that decision, did you find your-self still off course, so to speak, still running in the opposite direction from your intended purpose?

Through the most staggering events in life, athletes do what they've been trained to do: win. Pete Sampras, the con-summate tennis player, did what he was trained to do in 1994. While the world was watching the events surrounding a white Bronco and an ex-football player, Pete Sampras was winning the Australian Open and Wimbledon, doing what he was trained to do: win. In 2000, while the world was debating the US Presidential fiasco that took place in the Florida beltway, Tiger Woods was doing what he was trained to do: winning the US Open, British Open, and PGA Championship. Just winning.

After taking a moment to reflect on the importance and fragility of life after September 11th, 2001, Lance Armstrong hopped back on his bike carrying the hopes of millions of cancer patients with him and did what he was trained to do: beat cancer, beat pain, beat odds, and win his fourth Tour de France in 2002. In a world of complicated theories about suc-cess, athletes keep the purest process of winning alive and safe through tradition. Athletes surpass what the norms deem impossible, what the commentators label unfathomable, and what spectators view as dreams. These athletes all beat the impossible and so can you.

I, too, have beaten impossible. How? It wasn't the last shot Michael Jordan made in the 1998 NBA championship, securing the Chicago Bulls 2nd three-peat victory that inspired me. It wasn't young Tiger Woods' 1997 record-breaking triumph at the

Augusta National Golf course, where thousands stood watching a 21-year-old give minorities hope. My beating the impossible didn't make it to television. It didn't hit the newsstands nor the radio airwaves. Beating the impossible was overcoming every imaginable opponent and major hurdle to get to my destination.

I walked out of a seminar one day knowing I was supposed to be there, just like Michael Jordan knew he was supposed to make the winning shot with seconds left on the clock, like Tiger Woods who knew he was supposed to be the first minority to win the Masters, and like Lance Armstrong who knew he was supposed to beat cancer and win the Tour de France. That feeling of beating the impossible comes with an almost spiritual awakening that makes you question what actually is impossible, and who was the wise crack who said the word should not even exist?

When you have experienced beating the impossible, you look at the world and everything around you differently. You understand why President John F. Kennedy succeeded in his promise to the world on May 25th, 1961 to send an American safely to the moon by the end of the decade. You can identify with the attitude of Richard Williams when he declared to the tennis world that his daughters, Venus and Serena Williams, would dominate the sport in their prime. These people are all athletes, and they run, not towards average, not towards okay, but directly up to impossible and deal it a crashing blow.

Success is nothing more than a game, a high-stakes game, a closely contested journey of wins and losses. Either you're

playing or you're being watched; you're in control or someone is controlling you; you're a fan or an athlete. A game is a
competition that requires intense involvement and the only
questions worth asking and analyzing are, "Are you involved
in the game of your life? And if not, why not?" I'm sure
you've been playing in the lives of others, working for them,
giving your sweat, improving their quality of life. What
about yours—your dreams, your passions, your desires and
your wants? Are you ready to create your own event that
could take your breath away and leave you exhilarated and
hungry for the next challenge? That can happen if you're willing to break the impossible and make it possible, and that
will happen when you become an athlete.

COACHING YOURSELF TO WIN THE BATTLE

*"The key to coaching is not what you do, but the way
you do it. The intangibles, the motivational parts of
the game are the most important facets of it."*
—Rick Pitino Basketball Coach,
University of Louisville
(head coach of 1996 Kentucky
NCAA Championship Team)

*"Rarely is war won by one sweeping act of aggression.
Wars are won in series of battles, each victorious battle
the result of strategy, commitment, and risk."*
—Chapter 2, The Seven Battles in the War

The war of belief consists of a series of battles requiring application of the strategies necessary to ensure victory on every level. In the war of belief, you are both captain and soldiers, both coach and athletes navigating the strategy toward success and implementing that strategy in real time. A coach reacts to the rules of the game and creates the playbook needed to attain victory. You are a coach from the neck-up. This encompasses:

- **Self-Thought**
- **Self-Talk**
- **Self-Analysis**

Self-Thought: Self-thought represents what you feed your mind while in conversation with yourself. The most honest discussion takes place when no one is around. In the war, the coach has to intend to win in public, which comes with authentic intention in private. Intention is resolve, and resolve involves a declaration to win, to construct the mindset in your head which will produce victory. This is not based on feelings. This mindset creates the feelings you want to exhibit. Under any circumstances, you can produce the feelings by effectively fighting through the debris created in battle, while manifesting the victorious self-thought that produces victory's emotions.

Self-Talk: The right self-thought will produce the right self-talk, but having the right self-talk involves not only what you talk to yourself about, but what you talk to others about as well. A coach by trade is an intentional optimist. That doesn't mean he or she can't talk about the reality of the challenges in a battle, but it means that the angle of the conversation is to find the solution to reach the target. As a coach, one's conversation is to prolong wins, not to prolong whines. To tell the difference, ask yourself after the conclusion of your self-talk whether you formulated an internal strategy for victory or defeat.

Self-Analysis: If I asked you to name the top blunders, failures, and set-backs you've had in your life, how long would it take for you to summon them up in your senses? If I asked you to name your own top successes, top qualities, and top honors, will they come up just as quickly to your mind as the negative? Self-analysis is your ability to see yourself through the shade of brilliance and will affect how you see everything in the war of belief. This doesn't mean you will overlook improvements. In fact, looking at yourself through the shade of brilliance will make you more willing to look at areas within to improve because you will be analyzing yourself through the eyes of self-determination rather than self-condemnation.

As Rick Pitino highlighted *"The key to coaching is not what you do, but the way you do it."* The way you do it consists of the way you see you, the way you talk to you, and the way you access you. These factors will determine what you do in the war of belief. *"The intangibles, the motivational parts of the game are the most important facets of it."* The intangibles of the war of belief are self-thought, self-talk, and self-analysis.

THE COACH KEEPS THE GOAL IN MIND

"Have a vision. Sell your program. Your team is going to reflect you."

—Mark Gottfried, Basketball Coach,
University of Alabama

"While skill, resources, and ability no doubt play a role in winning the war of belief and accomplishing your goals, the first battle in the war is destination, meaning you must first buy into where you're going."

—Chapter 3: Battle 1,
Believing in Your Destination

The coach's vision has to be clear and focused on the goal at hand. The war of belief is about changing your life. Witnessing yourself make a 360-degree shift in mind, heart, and soul is absolutely one of the greatest feelings that life has to offer. Becoming a winner of the war is not only rare, it is legendary. It is proof that humans are indeed magnificent and that there are those consciously stepping out the shadows to prove it.

Your vision is not the finality. It is the spark. It creates the power of your planning and influences what you will consciously see in each battle. When your vision is clear, you can smell the aroma of victory, though surrounded by the stench of mediocrity. The vision opens the windows and allows fresh air to enter. That doesn't mean it changes the odor immediately, but it does start the process.

COACHING IS ABOUT WHAT YOU WANT TO BECOME

"Coaching is making people do what they don't want, so they can become what they want to be."
                                    —Tom Landry, Legendary ex-Coach
                                    of the Dallas Cowboys

"However, these things didn't come without sleepless nights, nervous days, and people looking at me peculiarly as I screamed to myself in the car encouraging myself to keep going."
                                    —Chapter 4: Battle 2,
                        Accepting the Fact that Belief is Unbelievable

Do you want this victory? Do you really want it? Then, be prepared to surrender what you want for what you want to become. This is the coach's creed—sacrifice, risk, and dedication. They have to become your mental motto. A new life is the Superbowl of life. Everyone has seen it, yet few have won it. Because the few start where others stop, stand while others sit, and act while other talk, the few do what they have to do now to live the way they want to live later.

As the Number One man at the movie box-office, Will Smith said on 60 Minutes, *"I'm not the most talented man in the game, but I have the sickest work ethic, while others sleep I'm up working, while they're partying, I'm mastering my craft."* That is the mentality of a winning coach. Others will chew gum while you chew pavement. This is the deal. Liking it is not even a question. Just get used to the answer.

COACHES COACH LIKE WINNERS FROM THE BEGINNING

"A person really doesn't become whole, until he becomes a part of something that's bigger than himself."
—Jim Valvano, Legendary Coach of the 1983 North Carolina State University NCAA Championship Team.

"You, the individual must be willing to change yourself to align yourself with victory in the war of belief in your life. You must understand that, yes, you do play the most crucial role in the process, not they, but you."
—Chapter 5: Battle 3, Establishing Your Belief Brand

Everyday wake-up handling every situation like a winner, regardless of where you are in life. This is a free exercise in life that will change your life. Become a part of something so huge, so ridiculously mind-blowing that it makes you nervous, excited, and scared. Shake-up your senses from the banal thoughts of the norm and dream without boundaries about where you want to go and what you want to become.

Look at setbacks as ways to test your winning mentality, to fight the comfort itch by refusing to go back and to bring your past into the present. Live in the minds of winning coaches. Feed your mentality winning ways so you can fortify the athlete within to produce winning action.

CHAMPION ATHLETES HAVE ONLY ONE OPTION . . . WINNING

> *"If money titles meant anything, I'd play more tournaments. The only thing that means a lot to me is winning. If I have more wins than anybody else and win more majors than anybody else in the same year, then it's been a good year."*
>
> —Tiger Woods,
> Ranked #1 PGA Golf Player

> *"Victory is yours. This war of belief has already been won by you. Right this very second, the victory in the war is yours to claim. What would you do at this point? Would you start looking around and taking visual inventory of what you've accumulated in life?"*
>
> —Chapter 6: Battle 4,
> Expanding your Belief Maze

You are a homerun hitter. You are not an average athlete participating in average things for average reward. You are a winner, you step to the plate to win, you think win, act win, breathe win, talk win, and react to keep winning. This is not about money. Money is a by-product of victory. This is about your own self-worth being increased daily by your willingness to fight the war.

What excites you is winning. That also must include excitement about the action used to produce the result of winning. No pain no gain, no sweat no glory, you have to put it all on the line for what you want to receive. This is the mark of a winner, the hallmark of your fighting this war of belief like a seasoned athlete.

ATHLETES WANT TO HAVE THE BALL IN THEIR HANDS

"If you run the ball, you control the clock. If you control the clock, you usually control the game."

—Tiki Barber,
Retired All Pro Running Back,
New York Giants

"To have freedom, you must become the authority on what you want. You have to become the CEO of your life. If you want the freedom of self-esteem, then you need to ensure your esteem hedges on you, that you can have access to that feeling. If you want financial freedom, then you need to have access to that process, have the skills to earn that freedom salary or be the person granting you access to pay yourself on a freedom scale. You want spiritual freedom? Then you had best have access to the giver of that freedom, access to study and

*navigate in the way the authentic freedom-holder
intended. Without access to the door that opens to your
dreams, your belief will not materialize, regardless of
how well-intended you are and regardless of your talent."*

—Chapter 7: Battle 5,
Understanding the Game within Belief

This is your ball, your show and your moment. You can't win the war if you don't want to put the ball in your court and maneuver around those trying to strip you away from it. It takes courage to get to the source. You have to demand access to your life, take control away from factors that are irrelevant to getting to your target and upgrade your selection to where you are going to focus your resources. Winning meaningless battles does nothing for winning the overall war.

You are the authority with the right, but don't look for people to give you the right immediately. You have to be willing to take what's yours, and, if necessary, take your self-esteem, your self-confidence, and your self-respect from those not willing to give it to you. This is your dream. Play it like it belongs to you.

ATHLETES DON'T FEAR FAILURE. THEY FEAR NOT FAILING

*"I've missed more than 9000 shots in my career. I've lost
almost 300 games. 26 times, I've been trusted to take
the game winning shot and missed. I've failed over*

and over and over again in my life. And that is why I succeed."

—Michael Jordan,
Voted the greatest NBA player
of all time by his peers and
national sports critics

"Athletes surpass what the norms deem impossible, what the commentators label unfathomable, and what spectators view as dreams. These athletes all beat the impossible and so can you."

—Chapter 8: Battles 6 and 7,
Believing Like a Coach and
Playing Belief Like an Athlete

While most people fear failing, athletes do not. This is because non-failure means one didn't try at all. The war of belief will have its share of battles, conflicts, setbacks and failures. You have to grow accustomed to the normality of it all. Big games come with big risk and big rewards for the winner and loser. You grow when you engage in the war of belief. While everyone else stands behind the caution tape, winners are investigating the process, understanding the rules, including the important rule that you have to be willing to fail in order to win.

This is not up for negotiation. This is the deal. All winners have failed and will continue failing. Because they want to win, you cannot have one without the others. You are the

athlete with the knowledge, the skill, and the mental forti-
tude to contend with this aspect of the war. In the time of
set-back, talk to your coach, make sure the intended optimism is there, and check your vision to ensure you're still
dialed-in to your target. Remind yourself this is about one
option, winning, which leaves you no other option but to get
up and get back into the middle of heavy battle so you can
claim victory in the war.

CHAPTER 9

BONUS BATTLE

Protecting Yourself from Belief Viruses

The war of belief is controversial. Anyone playing the game of success will have to deal with the side effects, blowback and repercussions of change, moving beyond the bounds of the belief maze, confronting unintentional pessimism, and believing the unbelievable is not something shared by the masses. Those of us fighting this war stand in the line of reality, seeking a new life, not just a new circumstance.

In the new life, in the realm of controlled thought, you will have the audacity to have a thought of your own, the nerve to actually proclaim you will have a life of intentional optimism, intentional abundance, and intentional happiness and not face the peril of the undecided who decide to stay stuck, complaining and blaming. You will have the unmitigated gall to stand up, bear witness in front of the all onlookers, and demand a new hand, this time shuffling your own deck.

New circumstances may occur in the battle, but this is not the end result. You may get a raise to help you get by, but your destiny is saying bye-bye to getting by and hello to increasing your assets, starting with your own self-value. You appreciate the apology from an unintentional pessimist who hurt your feelings inadvertently, but the end result is being the athlete playing the game of success so comfortably that when it happens again you don't even notice it, can't feel it, and really don't have time to reflect on it.

A new life is the reason we stand in the line. We've jumped out of the line around the building which is serving-up mediocrity. The war of belief puts you on stage, and in concert for all to see, to be studied, sometimes scrutinized, criticized, and tested. This is the final battle, in which you deal with the observers of your venture, those that stand in the sidelines sending various messages, some encouraging, and some cloaked in belief viruses that will test the stamina of your stance.

NEGATIVITY IS NOT AUTOMATICALLY A BELIEF VIRUS

Every adverse reaction to your decision to fight the war of belief is not the same reaction, so it doesn't carry the same purpose or intention. Nor does it have the same weight. This is important because fighting the war requires a great amount of exertion, so the energy spent on unnecessary concerns reduces energy to be used for seeking your target.

In the previous chapter, we were likened to a supercomputer. In that metaphor, action is comprised of the package of software that accompanied our entrance to life (*i.e.*, belief inheritance) and the programming input we as adults consciously choose to download *via* what we read, watch, listen to. Because our mentalities are easily exposed, everyone fighting the war of belief becomes susceptible to various belief viruses.

The all encompassing words "negative" and "negativity" do not necessarily constitute the belief virus in themselves. "Negativity" and "negative" have become the latest buzzwords to characterize all adverse response to a person's chosen course. Of course, there exist negative people whose concept and agenda is truly to bless the world with their unique dismal perceptions of everything progressive, different, or outside the cookie-cutter box of the professed norm.

However, soldiers of the war have to use negativity by avoiding blind broad assumptions. Some of the best advice I was given in the war has come from individuals who would have been perceived as "negative" by most. Truth can have a negative effect on your senses, and blunt truth is not for the delicate or weak. You want more, more will be asked of you, and in reality your perception of what is negative will be separate from how you feel.

Was it negative for a person to tell a young African-American man like myself that I am right about everything on my back, the racism, the injustice, the setbacks, but that nobody cares, that I should be a player, work out my legs, learn how to carry that weight with me, open my eyes and see I am not the only one in the locker room with regret, set-backs, or abuse who can claim them as legitimate reasons not to try? There are those like you clawing with your fingernails trying to make lemons out of lemonade. What is your intention?

That gut-check may seem negative to those more concerned with how they feel than with what is real. The reaction to what someone says is not necessarily the belief virus, especially if what they say is truthful and can be used to point you in the direction of your target. This is not based on who told you, how they told you, but what they told you. I will not subject myself to blatant disrespect. However, if the person has a questionable delivery method, yet their words have viable meaning in assisting me in winning the war of belief, I will listen, but they can hang up me remembering the names of their kids.

THE BELIEF VIRUS HAS MANY STRANDS

Wikipedia defines computer virus as follows:

> Some viruses are programmed to damage the com-
> puter by damaging programs, deleting files, or
> reformatting the hard disk. Others are not designed
> to do any damage, but simply replicate themselves
> and perhaps make their presence known by present-
> ing text, video, or audio messages. Even these benign

viruses can create problems for the computer user. They typically take up computer memory used by legitimate programs. As a result, they often cause erratic behavior and can result in system crashes. In addition, many viruses are bug-ridden, and these bugs may lead to system crashes and data loss.

Viruses as you can see are all different depending on the type. Every virus does not merit the same response. This is important to understand as you are fighting your war of belief. As stated before, the war requires a great amount of exertion, so the energy spent on unnecessary concerns reduces energy that can be use in hitting your target. There are no doubt formidable threats to your hard drive that require confrontation, but, as I will explain further, others may just need to be left to co-exist with the system and for personal virus blockers to handle.

The central reason we cannot call everything a threat is the simple fact we are athletes in this game of success, the target being the success we try our best to reach. We should restrain ourselves from quick knee-jerk responses to ensure we provide a tactical reaction to various viruses that may surface, one carried out with the end in view, specifically winning.

Really digest that for a second. Anything pertaining to winning is the end result to our response, the reason we even engage. That means we upgrade our reasons for response. I used to respond to every adverse comment to me with the same intensity, and, for that, as all hotheads, I've faced the consequences of those non-tactical reactions. What I didn't know then that I know now is that your value of self determines the value you place on what people say about you.

What I had then was no self-value which instantly maximized the value I placed on what people said about me. Everything felt like an attack on me. Metaphorically speaking, as it relates to my self value, I was standing in the middle of a Chicago snowstorm wearing nothing but a sleeveless shirt. It wasn't what was said, but my lack of mental clothing that made what was said that more stinging.

Below is the category of three viruses and the damage they can cause to your hard drive. We are going to categorize the viruses in three forms in order to equip ourselves with the response needed to nullify the danger they may pose to our hard drive.

Oppressors: This virus ' entire objective is to crash your hard drive. It cannot be resolved with reason. Major exertion may be needed to protect oneself from this deadly invasion.

Opinionated: This virus is not as harmful as it is oppressive. Its intent is not to cause a crash in your hard-drive. Unintentional pessimists can easily be opinionated, so can others who are not playing the game of success don't understand the history of the sport. Overextended energy needed to deal with this virus will definitely cause the system to slow and can lead to a hard drive crash.

Oppositional: This can have seemingly the same characteristics as an oppressive virus, yet be different. It presses a little deeper than opinionated and may actually oppose a stance to your hard-drive. It takes a bit more exertion to deal with than the opinionated virus, but it is not oppressive in nature because it comes with no clear intention to crash the hard drive. If not handled properly, this will eventually crash the hard-drive.

Characteristics of Damaging Viruses (Oppressors): *Damage program, delete files, reformate hard disk leading to system crash. Oppressors are red-lights due to the fact their intent is to crash your dreams.*

An Oppressor virus can be as subtle as it is brutal, leaving its mark on new soldiers embarking on fighting the war of belief. The oppressor is not data driven, hope driven, or dream driven. It is driven on crashing hard drives. Oppressor's agenda is to tear down, sometimes due to fear of a new belief which presents a threat to them. A strong hard-drive will usually crash from imput from weak, degrading software, which may pose a threat to the oppressor.

Although the oppressor has some of the same characteristics as opinionated and oppositional viruses, the oppressor has one clear distinction. Regardless what is happening on the battlefield, its meter of response usually stays the same, negative and/or condescending. This virus can reformat a strong hard drive and make it weak, delete files of self-esteem in seconds, and is never responsible for anything. This virus' intent is to crash. Period.

Characteristics of Benign Viruses (Opinionated, Oppositional): *Take up space/memory used by legitimate programs, cause erratic behavior, potentially cause system crash. Opinionated is a green-light virus. You could travel through it* *easily and not suffer damage to your hard-drive. Oppositional is a yellow-light virus. You must proceed with caution when dealing with this virus because you can sustain damage quickly if not careful.*

Opinionated

One of the definitions of "opinion" is *a belief stronger than an impression and weaker than positive knowledge.* Opinionated people can be likened to the effects of what happens when someone comes in making a great first impression. After the five-minute impression, the person leaves, and everyone talks favorably about the person. Hearing their opinions, you find that folks got a sense that the person knows them, *a belief greater than an impression.* Yet because the person was only there for five minutes and they can't truly know the person, *their belief is weaker than positive knowledge.*

Opinionated people are usually passionate about their impressions. Yet when the majority of them are questioned about those opinions, you soon find out that, although passionate, they lack serious positive knowledge. Some of the most passionate and opinionated objectors to my ventures have been people who never took the venture themselves, risked anything themselves or tried to break out of their own belief maze. Yet they offered me their very strong opinions about my chances for success based on an impression. They were not oppressive with the intent to crash the hard-drive. Most of them were very well intended, but in the process being unintentionally pessimistic.

Oppositional

These individuals may actually talk directly against your reasons for fighting the war of belief and may seem a bit hostile regarding your action of breaking out of the maze. They may have experience failure in their own venture or due to belief inheritance cannot see farther than where their lives have taken them. They may feed on every particular setback or failure that comes with going after a dream.

Their intent is not to crash your hard-drive. However, if you don't protect yourself, they will. Both the oppositional and opinionated viruses can take up space in a hard-drive, making the system forget its own strength. Both can consume a hard-drive's time and drain the energy of a hard-drive to the point that it cannot fully function on direct issues dealing with winning the war.

HOW A VIRUS SPREADS AND SELF-PREVENTION

Viruses spread from one computer to another to interfere with computer operation. Viruses are most easily spread by attachments in e-mail messages or instant messaging messages. That is why it is essential that you never open e-mail attachments unless you know who they are from and unless you are expecting them. Viruses can be disguised as attachments of funny images, greeting cards, or audio and video files.

Viruses also spread through downloads off the Internet. They can be hidden in illicit software or other files or programs you might download. To help avoid viruses, it is essential that you keep your computer current with the latest updates and antivirus tools, stay informed about recent threats, and follow a few basic rules when you surf the Internet, download files, and open attachments.

Once a virus is on your computer, its type or the method it used to get there is not as important as removing it and preventing further infection.

1 **Viruses spread from one computer to another to interfere with computer operation.**

PRINCIPLE: your circle of influence must be free of viruses

Your circle of influence should include the people that advise you to win the war of belief. These are the few key people in your life that have the resume that is needed to give you guidance in the battles. This group of individuals must be free of belief viruses, your selection of who will sit on this panel is key to your success.

Your friends and family may be great influences in other areas of your life, but if they have yet to break out of their belief maze and test the waters of risk and reward, they do not have the skills to be in your circle of influence. This is not an issue of right and wrong or one that should cause guilt. Remember, you are playing the sport of success. Some people belong in the stands, and some on the field. My family and friends can advise me on anything off the field. When they research, risk, experience, and deal successfully with the side-effects that come with this game, then based on their resume they will be in my circle of influence. This does not mean that you discount everything someone is speaking from the stands. If someone in the stands bring me advice based on someone that has played the game of success, then that conversation is a part of the relevant influence because it involves a winner who has played the game.

Belief viruses find openings, so if you, being a athlete in this game, look to the media (*i.e.,* those in stands watching to be your circle of influence), you will be subjected to information most of the time from individuals, however well intended, who have yet to play the game. If everyone in your life is in the stands, there are tons of books available about individuals whose stories about overcoming the war of belief can be your source of influence.

2 Never open AN e-mail attachment unless you know who IT IS from and UNLESS you are expecting it.

PRINCIPLE: always do credible checks before you input the software

THE WE TELL IT LIKE IT IS BLOG . . .

USERNAME: SPOOKYI
Did you hear about those Wright brothers trying to invent an object that flies, I heard they don't even get

*along, and check this out they didn't even go to
college . . .*

USERNAME: GIGGLES4EVER
*Just goes to show you how stupid people will follow any-
thing, a flying what they call it airplane.*

USERNAME: TAKEOVER
*You think that's something there's this guy trying to
create a device where people can talk to each other over
wires, his name is Alexander Bell . . .*

USERNAME: FREENCLEAR
*Yeah I heard of him, but you know his parents were
deaf so I just think he's suffering from that . . .*

USERNAME: GIGGLES4EVER
*Yeah he's suffering from somethingJ . . . people talking
through wires, what a hoot*

USERNAME: SEEMENOW
*Hey I heard that Rosa Parks didn't even sit on that bus
she was just tired and someone offered her the sit, my
brother who does dispatch for the bus company told
me . . .*

USERNAME: SPOOKYI
Really he was there?

USERNAME: SEEMENOW
*No, but his friend that drives for the same transit com-
pany that Rosa Park was on told him, he said his friend*

who was actually on the bus just before Rosa came on saw it while he was actually getting off . . .

Username: giggles4ever, spookyi, freeNclear

Wowwwwwwwwwwwww

One of the advisors in my circle of influence who investigates everything before inputting it in her hard drive relayed to me this nugget "people will live and die and their illusions." Information is key to the war of belief, credible, verifiable, information. Most of us come from a spoon-feed environment where information is told and accepted with few ever saying, wait a minute let me see that for myself.

The war of belief provided me with an escape from a belief system spoon-feed to me from birth. This war gave me the courage to seek out the founder of my particular belief. I was castigated, discouraged and subjected to fear used by unintentional pessimists who bought into the fear preventing them from acting to dig themselves out. Once I discovered my advisor's original writings, I awakened to a freedom I had never felt before in my life and the realization that if you don't know the original source of your beliefs, you're living at best, as my advisor declared, in an illusion.

If you're entering this game, you have to be prepared to take the heat, be prepared to question all information flow, have the courage to pick your advisor team and have the mental stamina to deal with the hits that come with navigating your own trail. Freedom is not free if you don't have access to your own choices. You had better check the resources that aided you in relinquishing them. If you do not check the software being sent to your hard-drive, you may have the computer set-up but someone else will be working your keyboard.

3 To help avoid viruses, it is essential that you keep your computer current with the latest updates.

PRINCIPLE: the factor is your immune system not the belief virus

Although susceptible to viruses of many kinds, the primary danger to the truth is not that viruses exist but more importantly that they feed off holes. Every belief virus feeds off the holes within a hard-drive. They will crash the hard-drive if the holes are not patched up and secured. You must understand that this one fact about your immune system is more important than the belief viruses.

In adjusting to the process of fighting the war of belief, like most people, I was great at looking at other people, blaming them, saying how unaccountable I was to my for situation. With that set-up, every belief virus I encountered crashed my hard-drive. However, once the focus shifted and I became that athlete unconcerned with the other team but concerned instead with my level play, the belief viruses may have stung at times but the crashing of the hard drive stopped. To shift the focus for yourself, do a basic checkup from the neck-up.

- What are you reading, talking about, and listening too?
- Who are your associates?
- Is your mind on the present or past?
- Are you playing like an accountable athlete?
- Are you talking to yourself like a coach or a fan?

Another hole we need to fill in most individuals harddrives is that they have no plan. They wake up without an agenda for their hard-drive and float through the day allowing life and whatever curves it throws to be the agenda. Inside those curves are belief viruses ready to lay dormant in harddrives left unprotected. Reacting to the curves in life becomes their agenda, during the day and in life. A life they don't control with belief viruses becomes their plan.

Patching up the holes and securing your immune system starts with waking up each day with an intention, a conscious determination to act according to your own objectives mentally, emotionally and physically. You should live to protect that intention daily, to prevent viruses from eroding your hard drive and from crashing your agenda to act in accord with your goals. Create your personal intentions and live by them. They represent your mental immune system. If you find yourself getting distracted, not living based on those intentions, a belief virus has invaded your senses.

- I intend to be secure in my right to succeed.
- I intend to guard my hard-drive and input what is needed for success.

- I intend to question before accepting and accept once truth is revealed.
- I intend to be optimistic, positive and fearless.
- I intend to rebound powerfully and positively from setbacks.
- I intend to recognize I am flawed and count not my failures but my moments of self-forgiveness.

Keep in mind that intention is resolve, and determination is to settle. If we combine the meanings, we resolve to settle all things in a manner leading us to our target. Having a target upgrades the response because winning for unprofitable means is meaningless and time wasted in non-profit confrontation is time that can be spent in the profitable inputting of necessary software. A strong immune system protects us, for the most part, from various belief viruses.

3 **Once a virus is on your computer, its type or the method it used to get there is not as important as removing it and preventing further infection.**

PRINCIPLE: the exit is more important than the entry

After taking all preventative measures to secure your hard drive, checking your immune system, checking the credibility of information, and securing your circle of influence, when the belief viruses invade and actually enter your hard drive, remember the exit is more important than the entry.

The belief virus distracts you from your target, regardless of its shape. The specialty of its entry mission is to distract. You have to be prepared to exit the situation, realizing that prolonged conversation about how the belief virus got inside your hard drive is counterproductive to the war of belief. It may give you a sense of relief to continue a great analysis on how the entry effected you, but remember you are an athlete moving at a fast pace toward success and time is valued as a premium.

Dwelling on the exit doesn't mean you become emotionless. It means that while reeling from the very real aspect of being invaded, you keep your eyes fixed on the target, recognizing that the invasion doesn't change the target but that it can change your intention at that moment potentially causing you to lose focus of the target.

Set-backs, failures, and unexpected events don't change the process of how the sport is played, but they do test the make-up of the athlete. As Kenneth Chenault, CEO of American Express, said and other athletes playing this game can attest to, "under crisis is when you see the character of a person."

To stay true to the program of exiting, have a mental plan prior to the invasion so as not to be swayed by the shock of the hit. Create five intentions you will have while under test, for example:

- I intend to play while uncomfortable.
- I intend to reflect on the target when things are unclear.
- I intend to look for advice from my circle of influence when under attack.
- I intend to reflect on the examples of players that have won the war under emotional and mental duress.
- I intend to respond only in a way that secures victory.

Plan your intention strategy while things are calm. Do not allow things to surprise your senses. Face the fact that belief viruses will come, that they have always attacked the sensibilities of those fighting the war of belief, and that victors of the war have nonetheless pressed on in spite of challenges because they had declared and were firmly fixed on the fact that the war was theirs to own and to win.

THE WAR IS YOURS...

I don't know the reasons you've entered the war of belief, but dreams are meant to be pursued by the fearless and navigated by the hearts of those willing to step out of the shadows of the norm and take on the challenge of change.

Maybe this is personal, your own desire to see yourself differently in the mirror, to consciously choose a change in your own direction instead of being sent to places you had no hand in picking for yourself. Maybe you would like to have the courage to ask a question instead being asked the questions in your life. Maybe this is about letting go of yesterday and bringing all your senses to the present, accepting for once that, yes, you have a right to anticipate the best, regardless of mistakes, regrets, and disappointments of years past or even yesterday.

Maybe you're fighting the war for the family, in the hopes of changing the tides of mediocre subservience to the life dealt to you unintentionally by parents who had it dealt to them. Maybe it's about seeing your children have their choice of dreams. Maybe its' about a friend, a spouse, a parent, a mission to give back to someone who has given you so much.

Individuals enter the war of belief for different reasons, with the reasons changing as the battles move full steam ahead. I entered the war because I needed something. At that time, I couldn't identify the specific something that I needed. All I knew then was that I didn't know joy, fulfillment, or personal contentment. As the battle pressed forward, my reasons expanded to include my mother, who fought with her lasting breath to give me a chance to have a chance. Then it became about my nieces and nephews, so innocently sketching out their images of life using the images surrounding them.

The war of belief became my faith to believe that someone greater than me loves me, smiles at me for fighting the greatest battle individuals past and present have fought, the right to be. Not to be what trends, traditions, or belief inheritance dictate, but to dream beyond the boundaries of the maze, redesigning the destiny for myself and my family for generations to come.

Make no mistake about it, this venture has come with its tears, setbacks, failures, jubilations, wins and loses. It has served up ridicule and introduced me to naysayers as well as to some of the most remarkable spirits dwelling in the hearts of people I've ever known. Ask me what strategy I used, I couldn't tell you. Ask me why that person was there that day to take my hand when I needed it taken, I couldn't explain it in such a way as to make you see it. Ask me how with nothing, something was created, you wouldn't be satisfied with the simplicity of my answer.

Maybe the war is not about asking questions, but about surrendering to an answer, the answer my mother gave me when I was a kid, that when I was created, the angels stood applauding the magnificence of my being. Act in the array of that glory. Construct your dreams in the splendor of the realization that the war doesn't start from the premise of "Can you win?" but instead with the question, "Can you start every battle acting, thinking, and responding to the answer already provided to you, that you are already a winner?"

ABOUT THE AUTHOR

J ULIUS HENDERSON is founder of You Consulting, a business consultant firm that provides management and customer service training to large and small-scale service oriented companies. In addition he personally coaches and trains thousands of entrepreneurs and business leaders annually on ways to adjust to change, teach change, and effectively handle the side effects that come with leading change, in life and business.

Julius Henderson has authored three books all dealing with different aspects of personal change. Titles include Why Kids Don't Have Heart Attacks: *7 Reasons Kids Have Fun While Adults Have Prozac, The Puzzle Maker: Putting the Pieces Together to Your Identity,* and *The Seventh Decision.* He currently resides in El Dorado Hills, Ca. A host of media outlets have featured Julius Henderson as guest expert on the subject of personal change including:

Fox -Morning News Oakland, Ca

NBC-Morning Show Los Angeles, Ca

ABC-Early Morning Show, Phoenix, AR

CBS-Early Morning Show, Memphis, TN

CNN-Early Morning Show, Atlanta, GA

First for Women Magazine

If you would like to book Julius Henderson for your next event contact us at

www.juliushenderson.com

or

www.iamyouinc.com